FINDING GOD

FINDING GOD

REV. JOSEPH T. SULLIVAN

Troitsa Books
New York

Coordinating Editor: Tatiana Shohov
Office Manager: Annette Hellinger
Graphics: Wanda Serrano
Book Production: Matthew Kozlowski, Jonathan Rose and Jennifer Vogt
Circulation: Cathy DeGregory, Ave Maria Gonzalez and Raheem Miller
Communications and Acquisitions: Serge P. Shohov

Library of Congress Cataloging-in-Publication Data

Sullivan, Joseph T.
Finding God / Joseph T. Sullivan.
   p.   cm.
Includes index.
ISBN 1-59033-197-4
1. Theology, Doctrinal – Popular works. 2. Catholic Church – Doctrines. I. Title.
BT77.S78   2002   CIP
230 – dc21   2001059619

Copyright © 2002 by Rev. Joseph T. Sullivan
   Troitsa Books, a division of
   Nova Science Publishers, Inc.
   227 Main Street, Suite 100
   Huntington, New York 11743
   Tele. 631-424-6682 Fax 631-424-4666
   e-mail: Novascience@earthlink.net
   Web Site: http://www.nexusworld.com/nova

All rights reserved. No part of this book may be reproduced, stored in a retrieval system or transmitted in any form or by any means: electronic, electrostatic, magnetic, tape, mechanical photocopying, recording or otherwise without permission from the publishers.

The authors and publisher have taken care in preparation of this book, but make no expressed or implied warranty of any kind and assume no responsibility for any errors or omissions. No liability is assumed for incidental or consequential damages in connection with or arising out of information contained in this book.

This publication is designed to provide accurate and authoritative information with regard to the subject matter covered herein. It is sold with the clear understanding that the publisher is not engaged in rendering legal or any other professional services. If legal or any other expert assistance is required, the services of a competent person should be sought. FROM A DECLARATION OF PARTICIPANTS JOINTLY ADOPTED BY A COMMITTEE OF THE AMERICAN BAR ASSOCIATION AND A COMMITTEE OF PUBLISHERS.

Printed in the United States of America

"…you shall seek the LORD, your God;
and you shall indeed find him
when you search after him
with your whole heart and your whole soul".
Deuteronomy 4:29

Imprimatur: Most Reverend Kenneth A. Angell, Bishop of Burlington

Censor Librorum: Reverend Michael J. St-Pierre

Granted: June 12, 2001

Contents

Introduction		xi
Chapter One	First Steps	1
Chapter Two	One God, Many Gods, Myths and Reality	5
Chapter Three	Does it Make a Difference?	9
Chapter Four	Messiah	13
Chapter Five	Acceptance	17
Chapter Six	Islam	21
Chapter Seven	Respect Not Rivalry	25
Chapter Eight	Ecumenism	31
Chapter Nine	Worship	35
Chapter Ten	Union with Christ	39
Chapter Eleven	The Human Condition	43
Chapter Twelve	Our Brothers and Sisters	47
Chapter Thirteen	The Fullness of Christ	51
Chapter Fourteen	Saints	55
Chapter Fifteen	Repent and Believe	59
Chapter Sixteen	God's Plan	63

Chapter Seventeen	Bits and Pieces	67
Chapter Eighteen	Acts, Habits and Character	73
Chapter Nineteen	A True Picture of Christ	77
Chapter Twenty	That You May Come to Believe	83
Chapter Twenty-One	A Sense of Awe	89
Chapter Twenty-Two	I Am the Resurrection	93
Chapter Twenty-Three	Encountering the Risen Christ	99
Chapter Twenty-Four	What Does All This Say to You?	105
Chapter Twenty-Five	Authority	111
Chapter Twenty-Six	Serving the Lord	115
Chapter Twenty-Seven	History, God's Intervention	121
Chapter Twenty-Eight	Timeline	127
Chapter Twenty-Nine	Church History	131
Chapter Thirty	The Church Grows	137
Chapter Thirty-One	The Middle Ages	143
Chapter Thirty-Two	Repercussion and Reform	147
Chapter Thirty-Three	Jesus Christ! Yesterday, Today and Forever	151
Chapter Thirty-Four	Freedom	157
Chapter Thirty-Five	Secularism	163
Chapter Thirty-Six	Side by Side	169
Chapter Thirty-Seven	Glory to God	175
References		181
Permissions		183
Index		185

INTRODUCTION

This book, *Finding God*, is meant for believers and nonbelievers. It is our hope and our prayer that this book will confirm and strengthen those who already have a good relationship with God. We hope and we pray too, that, with the grace of God, those who are unbelievers and those who are only nominally religious will come to know and to love God.

There are those whose religious education was only minimal. Perhaps they attended classes in a parish for a few years while they were growing up. Then, there were other demands on their time: school, extra curricular events, sports, hobbies, music and dance classes etc. So their formal education about God and his Church was sandwiched in and is limited. Occasionally they meet others who seem to have greater knowledge. They may wish to have a deeper understanding of God. There are questions they would like to ask. There is a longing within them to grow closer to God. They may welcome the opportunity to coordinate what they already know. *Finding God* hopefully will assist them to get a handle on life and to lead them into a more secure relationship.

Finding God is an easy reader, formatted into questions and answers. Maybe the book is not everything you always wanted to ask about religion, but it may just cover some of the subjects and issues.

At a point in time in the history of our world the heavenly Father sent his Son, Jesus Christ. Jesus said to Philip, "Whoever has seen me has seen the Father." (John 14:9) Christ is the best teacher. He shows the way and sets the example.

"I sought the LORD, who answered me, delivered me from all my fears. Look to God that you may be radiant with joy…". Psalm 34: 5-6

"Ask and it will be given to you; seek and you will find; knock and the door will be opened to you", Matthew 7:7

Chapter One

FIRST STEPS

I don't think much of religion. You're churchgoer. What makes you tick?
Why this negative impression of religion? Somebody rub you the wrong way?

Some people masquerade in holiness. Then, they get unmasked as hypocrites and cheats. Their scandals are reported in the news. Television personalities call for money in God's name. They skim the donations for themselves. Others lead double lives. Their bad example belies the morality they preach.
The media is quick to report on scandals. And if good people are being scammed, the media does us a service to expose the wrongs. The media reports on the sensational, the unusual, whatever qualifies as news. The media says if they report on the ordinary, it would be boring.

So you think my impression is inaccurate? Is it unfair to judge religion based upon those who are unfaithful to their religious profession? There are many who believe that religion is just a waste of time. Exposing the phonies tends to dispose us that way.
Some years ago there was story entitled, The Ugly American. I did not read it. I believe episodes ran in a magazine. Nevertheless, let's suppose that some of our citizens go on vacation, visit other lands and tour other countries all the while making themselves obnoxious. It is quite unfair to

judge all Americans by the distasteful conduct of a few travelers. Most churchgoers sincerely try to please God.

Many of us are on the outside looking in. There isn't a lot to go on. Impressions sink deep. There are millions of people whose families never bothered with religion or church attendance.

That's true. A priest drove into a church parking lot one morning. He started to climb the stairs leading to the back entrance. A little boy, perhaps six or seven years old, skated over to him on roller blades. The priest had never seen him before.

"I've never been in church", the little fellow declared.

The priest looked at him and said, "You are welcome."

"My grandmother doesn't take me", he replied.

"Your grandmother is welcome, too", said the good Father.

"I don't live around here", the boy explained. Then, he named a town some sixty miles away.

"Well, there are churches there", the priest assured him.

"Yeah, but they don't take me," said the boy.

Multiply that situation a few million times and there are many folks who have never had a church experience.

I honestly do not feel the need to have a religion. I've been okay up until now. I see men, women and children driving to churches. I've even attended a few services.

Still there is a need. You do have a need. It hasn't been brought home to you to date. But there will come a day. God has created us for himself. He is our destiny. Inevitably God is our ultimate goal in life.

You make me chuckle. Imagine me getting religion! How will this come about?

You may experience the emptiness of life. Years ago there was a war movie. Some scenes showed the devastation of bombing. Towns and cities were reduced to rubble. Eventually those who survived returned to their neighborhoods. There was nothing there. Their homes, shops, parks, roads, gardens…everything that was part of their lives, was gone. Family members and friends were dead. The world as they knew it was changed. At that time they needed inner resources, something to cling to. Despair

covered them like a blanket. Why go on living? How would they ever rebuild their villages and towns? How would they rebuild their own lives?

I can imagine what it was like. Even now tornadoes rip through areas of our country. People lose all of their possessions. They do need something to energize them. The kindness of friends helps a lot.

And what moves friends to share? For some it may just be humanitarian motives. Others are impelled by their faith in God. They are imbued with the commandments to love God and to love those around them. Have you ever thought how different this world would be if people lacked the higher motivation that comes from religion? We live in a civilized country, thanks to the faith that radiates in the minds and hearts of citizens. What a miserable place this would be if every person lived only for himself. "I've got mine. You get yours." Dog eat dog! "Might makes right." Fear, violence and misery would prevail.

So you think that collectively churches change help to the landscape. This is a kinder, gentler nation because of them? Unwittingly we underestimate the contribution faith-filled people make?

The answers to life's most serious questions come from religion. The reason for living itself flows from religion. "Raison d'etre", the very reason for existence, finds it answer from God's purpose in creating. Those who do not know God struggle to discover meaning. In times of crisis they flounder. Everyone needs inner resources and these come from religion.

I would think that belief, a faith, makes a great difference if some one was tempted to commit suicide. There are circumstances which appear insurmountable. People experience futility and frustration. They feel trapped. There is no way out. "Stop the world. I want to get off." They try to escape by taking their own lives. Pressing troubles, sorrow, pain, fear and distress are left behind, at least as they reason.

But there is always a way out. God's grace is sufficient in every situation. It is possible to overcome the odds. Knowing God, the religious person realizes that only God has absolute dominion over life. He says when we come into this world. He says when we are to leave this world. This is God's divine prerogative. The man or woman under severe strain

is strengthened and comforted. Loving God means embracing his holy will. Saints come to perfection, often through their sufferings. They do not even consider taking their own lives. During the first three centuries of Christianity, Christians were martyred for their faith. You can see that their perspective differs from the perspective of unbelievers.

Yes, believers are different. Their lifestyle is different. Their characters are formed with a spiritual dimension. I guess that's why I am curious. They live and act differently. What is the hidden ingredient? Tell me why religion inclines them so.

To put it simply, God is the object of their lives. They recognize a Supreme Being. They bond with God. They develop a relationship. They are like an arrow heading straight for the target.

Of course, there are religions and there are religions. Colleges and universities teach courses comparing religions. In this academic approach students may just be confused. A godless professor may scoff at the whole confusing conglomeration. The starting point of the courses may be that religion is an invention of various races. They react to the forces of natures. Perhaps the inhabitants of this planet began to worship a sun god, or a rain god, or a god of fertility. Students may form the opinion that religion, or religions, have developed through the ages with people reacting to their surroundings and experiences.

To be true, religion has to be a relationship with the one, true God. There is a history of different people relating to many gods, to many systems. The Greeks and Romans had their gods. The Jews encountered false gods in their journeys and in quest for the Promised Land. But God himself clarified his relationship. People wandered off in many directions. God intervened. He showed the way. He defined the relationship.

Chapter Two

ONE GOD, MANY GODS, MYTHS AND REALITY

If God defined the relationship people ought to have with him, why did he wait so long? Centuries are filled with myths and forms of religion differing from one another, from country to country, and from continent to continent. If a person were coming in from another planet, he would be thoroughly bewildered. The whole thing is a big blur for me.

You are not really coming in from another planet are you?

Just joking!

At the start of creation, the beginning of the world, there was great harmony and coordination. You know the story of Adam and Eve. Through their sin, their defiance of God's will, everything turned topsy-turvy, so to speak. Among the consequences, they not only lost their innocence, but blessings called preternatural gifts. Their minds were darkened and their wills were weakened, all part of the chaos that ensued. God promised a redeemer, one who would restore the relationship. However, God did not specify the time and place, nor how he would accomplish this.

It is very hard to comprehend the long delay. If there is one, true God, why let centuries go by with populations not knowing how to respond to a single Supreme Being?

Living at this time in history many of us expect nearly instantaneous action. Americans want it all done yesterday. We react according to the wonderful technological advances: radio, television, film, press, computers, internet, e-mail, fax, whatever. St. Peter gives us something to think about. "But do not ignore this one fact, beloved, that with the Lord one day is like a thousand years and a thousand years is like one day.""2 Peter 3:8 God sees things from a different perspective. God is all knowing. He sees the past, the present, and the future at a glance.

This is overwhelming, a bit beyond us. We can only think in human terms because we are human.

And God who creates human beings knows how best to communicate with them. God speaks our language. All languages! In his infinite wisdom God knows when and how to communicate. His timing is perfect. For us to understand and appreciate, we have to tune in and attune our wave length. God knows the precise time when people are receptive. He works harmoniously with the freedom of the mind and the will.

What happened to the countless numbers of people who lived for centuries believing in these myths? Some myths seem rather farfetched and incredible today, even childish. Were people able to attain what we call heaven? I think it is safe to say that most people have some sort of belief that includes life after death.

There is no information or revelation about those who entertained religious myths in ancient days. God could recognize the sincerity of their lives, although their beliefs were not accurate. It is possible that they could have what we call "baptism of desire". This means they followed their consciences to the best of their abilities. In effect they would have followed the one, true God if they knew about him. This is a judgement beyond us. Nevertheless we might speculate in their favor relying on the compassionate mercy of God. Who knows?

History shows that mythology was widespread, spanning continents. Did people entertain myths because there was nothing else to go on? Was it the fear element, attributing supernatural powers and entities to forces they could not control like lightening and thunder and earthquakes?

There are all kinds of theories on how mythologies developed. The Greeks recognized six gods and six goddesses, the top god being Zeus. The Romans had three principal gods: Jupiter, Mars and Quirinus. After contact with the Greeks and suffering their influence, the Romans featured Jupiter, Juno and Minerva. There is a Pacific Island mythology and an African mythology. Irish and Celtic and Teutonic, too. Columbus and other explorers discovered that the American Indians had gods based on nature. Hernando Cortes, the Spanish conquistador, who conquered the Aztecs in 1521 learned of their many gods. Among the practices of the Aztecs there were human sacrifices.

Are there common threads?

There appear to be resemblances from continent to continent. Looking at the whole picture. It seems that people gleaned insights from their surroundings. They attributed these to higher beings. Researchers reduce the myths to "creative" and "explanatory". They focused on the origin and birth of the gods and goddesses. And they focused on the possible rationale underlying sickness, death etc.

How about the Egyptians? Their history goes back a long way.

Travelers and tourists look at the pyramids and the Sphinx. Egyptian gods took the form of humans at times. Then, gods came in the form of animals. The dog or jackal represented Nubis. The Sphinx is a combination of both human and animal.

And there are some races and religions that regard some animals sacred today.

The challenge is on-going. In ancient times there were people who believed in many gods. The same can be said for the people living today. St. Paul wrote of this, warning Timothy, his friend and fellow evangelist. He encouraged Timothy to be faithful and authentic in his teachings about Christ. "For the time will come when people will not tolerate sound doctrine but, following their own desires and insatiable curiosity, will accumulate teachers and will stop listening to truth and will be diverted to myths." 2 Timothy 4: 3-4

And that was centuries ago. Human nature remains the same. The problem, too?

"What goes around, comes around", so they say. St. Peter said "We did not follow cleverly devised myths when we made known to you the power and the coming of our Lord Jesus Christ, but we had been eyewitnesses of his majesty." 2 Peter 1: 16 The apostle was saying that the early Christians had more to go on than myths. Their faith was based on fact and reality.

Well, who worships the one, true God today? There are still many religious systems.

Among the multiplicity of religions in the world there are eight major faiths. Buddhism has 108 different names for gods. Shinto speaks of a "Sky Father" and an "Earth Mother", Izanagi and Zanami. Those who profess Confucianism speak of Confucius, Shang-Ti. Taoism looks to the Jade Emperor and many folk gods. Hindu believers refer to Brahman, All Reality. And the other three major religions worship the same, one God.

And what are those three religions?
Judaism, Islam and Christianity.

This is getting a bit complicated.
You can imagine the challenge of someone starting from scratch and trying to sort it all out.

Some parents do not rear their children in any religion. They say they want their sons and daughters to choose for themselves.

And that is truly a formidable task. At least if they were brought up in one faith and in one tradition they would have something to build upon. They would have something to compare. Those mothers and father speak cavalierly as if they were champions of freedom. But they are hardly doing their offspring a favor.

Moslems follow Islam. They believe in Allah, do they not? Is Allah the one, true God?
Yes! The Moslems call God, Allah. The Jews call God, Yahweh. And Christians say God.

Chapter Three

DOES IT MAKE A DIFFERENCE?

Does it really make any difference what religion a person follows?
Of course! People are en route to God. They are in search for truth and for happiness. Ultimately they seek God. The way should be true.

Sometimes people say, "We are all going to the same place. It doesn't matter what you believe."
There are a lot of cliches around. If you examine them carefully, you can see that they do not have valid foundations. These are slogans that are passed around. In time they come to be somewhat accepted.

Well, are we all going to the same place, namely heaven?
Destiny is not automatic. God creates us with free wills. We can choose to follow and to obey. We can chose to do otherwise. It isn't written anywhere in the bible that everyone is going to heaven.

Often folks say, "It doesn't matter what you believe. It's how you act that counts."
This does not make sense. We act according to our beliefs and convictions. An atheist does not believe in God. An agnostic declares that it is not possible to know God. Their convictions could be diametrically opposed to the convictions of religious people. The cliché does not hold water. It is a gratuitous assumption. What is gratuitously assumed, may be gratuitously denied.

Nevertheless you have to admit that someone looking at the wide array of religious systems that exist, may be tempted to throw up his hands in despair. A man or a woman might spend a lifetime searching, testing, experiencing, and going from one religion to another.

The search for truth is worth it. The search for God is worth it. Eternal life and destiny hangs in the balance.

Do we know what truth is? And are we capable of knowing truth?

Yes! To both questions! You may recall that when Jesus Christ was standing before the Roman governor, Pontius Pilate, Christ said that he came to this world to bear witness to the truth. Jesus faced death. He faced Pilate's decision to hand him over for crucifixion.

One of the charges made against Jesus was that he claimed to be a king. Christ said the charge was true, but his kingdom was not of this world. "Then you are a king?" Christ replied, "You say I am a king. For this I was born and for this I came into this world, to testify to the truth. Everyone who belongs to the truth, hears my voice." Then Pilate scoffed, "What is truth?" (John 18: 37-38)

What makes truth, truth?

It is the conformity of the mind with what is outside the mind. It is acknowledgement of reality. If I tell you the bible is a motorcycle, you will say this is absurd. It is a book, or a collection of books. If I say that rain does not make you wet, you will say this belies reality. A lie is a falsehood. All of us are capable of knowing truth. Parents teach their children to tell the truth, to be honest. We know from experience what makes truth, truth.

It would seem that if God wanted everyone to know the truth about himself, he would have made it a lot easier.

God does not make mistakes. The difficulty of arriving at truth lies in the mind and heart of each person. The detrimental effect flows from original sin. Besides the approach to God is not merely intellectual. There has to be conformity to God's will. This is incapsulized in the preaching of John, The Baptist. Jesus said the same. Repent! And believe! Notice that "repent" comes before "believe".

The Lord knows precisely what it takes for a person to have a sincere and valid relationship with him. God provides the grace of conversion to all seek him without strings attached.

What about Judaism, Islam and Christianity? The same true God! Different systems?

Yes! However, there is a need to understand that religion is not just a system, or many systems. There is a dynamic involved. God intervened in history. God initiated the relationship. There is a vitality present even to this day. God is with us. Emmanuel! That's what the word means.

You mean that God is running our world?

In a sense, yes! That delicate balance between almighty God and empowered humans goes on. In one way nothing happens unless God concurs. In another way, we are the "masters of our fate and the captains of our souls". Having created us with free wills, God respects his own creation. God allows us to act freely, his divine providence notwithstanding.

Tell me about Judaism.

Judaism, the word, comes from Judah, one the tribes of Israel. There were twelve tribes among the Jews. The word, Jew, comes from the word for Hebrew, which was the language the people spoke.

God spoke with a man named Abram. He lived near the mouth of the Tigris and Euphrates Rivers, in a land once called Mesopotamia (between the rivers). Today the area is located in southern Iraq. God made a pact, or covenant, with Abram about 1850 B.C. His name was changed to Abraham, meaning "the father of many nations". Abraham was chosen because he believed in the one God. There were many gods honored by the peoples and nations that existed then. God would be the God of Abraham and his descendents. They would be his people. It was a privileged and singular relationship. This was unprecedented in the history of the world.

So Judaism had its start with God intervening in the world. Given the existence of many people and many nations, this relationship appears exclusionary.

In a sense this seems true. I like the adjectives: singular, special and chosen. I don't think the God wrote off the rest of the world. But his dealings with humans were centered with the Jews. God promised to give Abraham and his descendents a land, the Land of Canaan. The bible tells of their journeys, their wanderings, and their conflicts with the peoples and the countries en route to the Promised Land. This territory is looked upon as the eastern end of the Mediterranean Sea, modern Israel.

So the religion is tied up with a particular people, the Jews, and a particular place, the Promised Land.

Yes! History and relationship with God is interwoven. God's covenant with Abraham was renewed many times over the centuries with the Jews. In 1250 BC God promised, through a great leader named Moses, "...you shall be my special possession...". (Exodus 19:5) This was on Mount Sinai. God spoke to Moses there, proclaiming his Ten Commandments, articulating the relationship between himself and the Jews.

Besides the Ten Commandments, how did God want his people to relate?

The specifics are summarized in what is called the Old Testament. This includes what the Jews call the Torah and the Talmud. These explain liturgy, worship, sacrifice, prayer. They have to do with daily living, observances in the Temple and at home. And all through the centuries there was a great expectation. God promised to send a Messiah. The Messiah would lead them into a more perfect relationship with their God. The biblical prophets told of the joy and delight that would come with the Messiah. The expectation of this Redeemer is dominant and essential in the fabric of their belief.

Chapter Four

MESSIAH

Just what is a messiah?

A messiah is considered to be a liberator, a deliverer, one who is instrumental in freeing people from oppression and injustice.

Many people in history would qualify under that definition.

That's true. In modern times Martin Luther King Jr. might be called a messiah. Do you remember his speech in the nation's capital. "Free...free at last...". He worked and prayed that African Americans would no longer be slaves in fact in a country which defeated slavery more than a century before. Then, Mikael Gorbachev and Boris Yeltsin helped to raise the Iron Curtain in Russia. There were leaders in several communist countries who fought for liberation. Simon Bolivar (1783-1830) in South America lead a revolution to bring it freedom from Spain.

Didn't the Jews have several messiahs or liberators in their long history?

On their way to the Promised Land they encountered many forms of injustice and oppression. They battled the Hittites, the Jebusites, the Canaanites, the Philistines...You must recall the story of young David, the shepherd, slaying the giant, Goliath, a Philistine. Because God was on David's side, he stung the giant with a stone from a sling, and then, decapitated the Philistine with the man's own sword.

Moses must be held in high esteem for leading the Hebrews from their slavery in Egypt.

With God's grace, Moses brought the Jews out of the land of their captivity. The Red Sea parted for them. Moses encouraged them to persevere during their forty years of wandering through the desert. Through Moses God renewed the covenant that he made with Abraham and his descendants.

The Jews were sustained through the preaching of their prophets when they lived in exile. There was hope and there was expectation that God would be with them, that they would eventually succeed. Many prophets spoke about The Messiah. Each generation looked forward to the Messiah's arrival.

Did the one and only Messiah ever come?
Yes!

And who is he?
Jesus Christ!

But Christ did not lead his people to freedom from oppressors. He was not a revolutionary. Even those of his day did not see him extricating them from the heavy hand of the Romans. His place in history is not characterized in the same manner as the other "messiahs".

True! The Hebrews were expecting a different kind of liberation, at least some of them. Their vision was limited to this world. It did not have the dimension of eternity. Christ restored the loving relationship that existed before original sin.

Jesus emphasized this when he declared to the Roman governor, Pontius Pilate, "My kingdom does not belong to this world". John 18: 36 Christ delivered all mankind from slavery to sin. He liberated everyone from the humanly inextricable guilt that resulted from disobedience to the heavenly Father's holy will. He remedied a relationship that once was loving. The infinite God was offended. Christ took upon his shoulders the cross of redemption.

This is a bit difficult to understand. We were focused on the Jews. And now you are speaking of Jesus Christ as the Messiah for the whole world.

Exactly right! The history of the world has to do with the history of the Jews. This is played out in the bible, both in the Old And New Testaments. It is through the Jews that God decided to intervene in the world. For centuries, from Abraham to Christ, God related to them and they related to God. It was an active, on-going relationship. But at a point in time, more than 2000 years ago, the heavenly Father sent his Son, Jesus. The special, often regarded as exclusive, relationship of God with his creatures, was extended to embrace everyone, all mankind. This is a loving gesture exceeding all expectations.

Does this include every person who ever lived? Is Christ the Messiah for everybody past, present and future? How is this possible?

It is possible. And it is true. The greatest event that ever took place since the beginning of the world was the coming of Jesus Christ. This is the divine plan. It is mind-boggling. When folks begin to grasp its significance, they are overwhelmed by the magnanimity of God's love. This is almost unbelievable. But, of course, it is true, and verified by what has taken place. The love of God, experienced by men, women and children, begets love in their hearts.

How is Christ capable of doing what other messiahs were not able to do in the past?

Jesus is not merely a man. He is truly God and man, one divine Person.

You mean Jesus Christ is God?
Yes!

How can this be? If Jesus was a man, how can he be God? Are you saying that a creature became the Creator?

No! I am saying that the Creator became a creature, that God became man. And this was without losing his divinity.

I don't know how you can say this. This defies logic.
In one way, this is mysterious. In another way, it is quite clear.

Explain!

This is called the Hypostatic Union. This is the unique union of human nature and divine nature. Jesus is one Person, a single unit of operation. Jesus is a divine Person, both God and man.

There is an axiom, an axiomatic expression, that may be helpful in understanding. "Agere sequitur esse." "To act follows to be." Everything that exists acts according to its nature. It can not be otherwise. You and I act like humans because we are human.

Jesus was human and acted like a human. He was divine and acted like God. Jesus demonstrated his divinity. He likewise demonstrated his humanity.

All this is in the bible?

Yes, of course! Jesus had a human mother, named Mary. He ate and drank and walked and talked. He suffered pain, hunger and thirst. All things that you and I do, were things that Jesus did. His birth took place in Bethlehem. He grew up in Nazareth. He died in Jerusalem. Jesus embraced the little children when they came to him. He touched people, like a blind man, whom he cured. He dined with Matthew and Martha and Mary and Zaccheus. He wept when he learned of the death of his friend, Lazarus. There is no doubt that Jesus was human.

What about being God?

Jesus did things that only God can do. His miracles are many and varied. Jesus multiplied a few loaves of bread and a few fish and fed thousands of people. This was on more than one occasion. He walked on the water and calmed stormy seas. The blind were cured and gained sight. The lame and the paralyzed walked. The deaf heard. Jesus called Lazarus, the daughter of Jairus, and a widow's only son back to life. Only God has power over life and death. Jesus said, "I and the Father are one". He proved his divinity. He acted according to his divine nature. "To act follows to be." "No one can give what hasn't got." Jesus had supernatural powers.

Chapter Five

ACCEPTANCE

If this is true, it is earthshaking. To say this is momentous is a gross understatement. God becomes man! Jesus is the Messiah! Let's back this up a bit. The Jews were God's chosen people. They were expecting a messiah. But when he came, they did not accept him. Am I correct? Jesus is not accepted as the messiah? Where does that leave us?

In their history the Jews expected a messiah who would deliver them from injustice. The Messiah would bring peace and prosperity. Many of their prophets were considered as messiahs because they bolstered the people's spirits. The prophets brought hope by their preaching. In time there was an expectation that the Messiah would be a descendent of King David. There were prophecies about the coming Messiah.

But Jesus was not accepted. Did he fail to fulfill the prophecies in their eyes? Were they looking in the wrong direction?

Hindsight is often better than on the spot judgement. Some of the people thought that there would be a personal Messiah. Others believed that there would be a period of blessing, a messianic age. Considering Jewish history these expectations must have seemed plausible to them.

If they were God's chosen people, why did they have endure such great hardships and suffering.

God was with them in many of their battles. They attributed their successes to the power of God. But it is true that they were enslaved and

persecuted. You will have to ask God for an explanation. God does not make mistakes. His rationale often escapes us. In 722 BC they were dominated by Assyria. Then, in 587 BC they were exiled to Babylonia. Persian King Cyrus and his armies conquered Babylonia in 539 BC. In 331 BC Alexander, the Great, conquered the Persians. The Romans, who conquered the world as it was known in ancient times, ruled Israel in 63 BC. The Romans were in control when Jesus was born.

But are you saying that they did not recognized God when he made a personal appearance in this world?
Some did come to believe in Jesus. Some did not believe that he was the Messiah. They did not believe that he was God.

You are telling me all this as background to explaining the three religions who believe in the one, true God? Judaism, Islam and Christianity?
Yes! The picture should come clear as we go along.

Why was Jesus rejected?
Jesus came to define and refine the relationship between the Jews (and all people) and the heavenly Father. He came, as Christ declared, to fulfill the will of his Father. The Jews related to God principally in accord with the Mosaic Law.

You mean the Law of Moses?
Jewish tradition attributes the first five books in the Old Testament of the bible (the Pentateuch) to Moses. God revealed them to Moses. Jesus said he came not to destroy the law, but to bring it to perfection. So he encountered conflict with the religious establishment of the day. He called for change in the manner that people related to God. His lifestyle and preaching was in collision with the embodiment of religion as it was observed.

Specifically how?
Among the ways emphasized in the New Testament were the observance of dietary laws and the association with people who did not observe the laws with purity. One incident singled out by the Pharisees was the failure of Jesus and his followers to wash their hands. This was

not merely an hygienic requirement, but a religious one. But, in fact, the law originally pertained to the priests and not everyone. In other words, as time went on, the Mosaic Law became extended and distorted.

This does not seem so terribly important.

It was important to the Jews. Jesus also dined with those who were considered to be sinners, tax collectors and the like. This was a "no no". The Pharisees complained. As time went on, they sought out occasions to discredit Jesus. They asked trick questions. But this strategy was no match for his simple and profound answers. The Pharisees prided themselves on the strict observance of the Mosaic Law. This was to show how religious they were. Confrontations took place. John, the Baptist, characterized the Pharisees as a "brood of vipers". Christ called them hypocrites.

Nevertheless this does not seem to be such a big deal.

Tensions mounted. Another party, the Sadducees, opposed Christ, too. They did not believe in immortality. Unlike the Pharisees, the Sadducees accepted only the written Law of Moses, and excluded the oral law. Then, there were scribes, who were like lawyers, learned in the Mosaic Law. Some regarded the strict observance of the law as oppressive. Jesus said, "Come to me, all you who labor and are burdened, and I will give you rest. Take my yoke upon you and learn from me, for I am meek and humble of heart; and you will find rest for yourselves. For my yoke is easy, and my burden light." Matthew 11:28-30

So Jesus did not live up to the expectations that some had about the Messiah. Yet. there were numerous prophecies, specifics about the one and only Messiah who was to arrive on the world scene.

God inspired biblical writers to set down particular details about the Messiah through the centuries. Prophecies abound. They include the time and place of his birth, his divinity, and the virginity of his mother, Mary. Christ was born in Bethlehem, which was the place where David lived. Both Mary, and her husband, Joseph, were of the tribe of David. The Holy Family, (Jesus, Mary and Joseph) fled in exile to Egypt when King Herod sought to kill the newborn Christ. Isaiah, the prophet, speaks of the ""suffering servant", referring to the Messiah. Christ's scourging,

mockery and agony were predicted. There were references to his crucifixion, burial and resurrection.

Are you saying that the people of Christ's day did not put it all together? They failed to coordinate the prophecies and relate them to Jesus?

It is easier now, historically speaking, after the facts, to see more clearly. Scripture scholars and theologians clarify and articulate the prophecies. Jesus, too, made prophecies which found fulfillment. He communicated about his passion, death and resurrection. Judas would betray him. Before the cock crows twice, Jesus said, Peter would deny him three times. The Holy Spirit would come down upon the early Church and activate the disciples. The magnificent temple of the Jews in Jerusalem would be destroyed. The Romans decimated the temple stone by stone in the year 70 AD. Christ declared that God's "Good News", the gospel, would be preached beyond Israel…to the entire world.

This is impressive, persuasive and conclusive. But why was Christ put to death?

His own people accused him of blasphemy, a serious charge. They brought him before the Jewish religious court, the Sanhedrin. False witnesses testified against him. The truth of the matter was that he did claim to be God. He proved this, demonstrating his divinity by countless miracles and healings. The charges against Jesus were altered when he was forced to stand before the Roman governor. Pontius Pilate would not have entertained the accusation of blasphemy, a religious matter. So Jesus was accused of subversion, inciting rebellion, and claiming to be a king. Nowhere in the New Testament are the charges verified. Jesus was truly "meek and humble of heart".

So he was crucified, hung on a cross until he died.

Christ's gesture was unspeakable. He offered the last drop of his precious blood for the salvation of every person on earth. He paid the price of the sins of every person past, present and future. He opened the gates of eternity. No one has ever shown greater love. The crucifix is the greatest symbol of God's love for us.

Chapter Six

ISLAM

The price of sins of every person past, present and future? Jesus was only one person. How was he able to take on the sins of the whole world? What you are saying signifies a stupendous and overwhelming dimension.

Exactly! Jesus is the one and only mediator between heaven and earth. He is the Messiah, the liberator, the savior of everyone. As a divine Person, Christ is equal to the heavenly Father. He is also equal to the Holy Spirit. As a human being, Christ took our guilt upon his shoulders. He represents us all.

There is only one God. But God has revealed that there are three divine Persons, the Father, the Son, and the Holy Spirit. God explained this about himself. We will talk about this mystery a little later on. The Father is God. The Son, Jesus, is God. And the Holy Spirit is God. This is called the Trinity. There is only one God, but three divine persons in the one God.

It is helpful to take this slow and easy. There is much to understand and coordinate. So far it appears that Christianity evolved or developed from Judaism.

Christianity flowers from Judaism insomuch as God enhanced the relationship with the Jews and brought it to perfection. The relationship between God and his human creatures is alive and dynamic.

Tell me about Islam. The Mohammedan believes in the same one, true God. What is the status of Jesus Christ in that religion?

Jesus is considered a prophet like the Old Testament prophets, Isaiah, Jeremiah, Ezekiel and others. He is not recognized as being divine.

Well, this is a fundamental difference between Christianity and Islam. There is a tremendous difference being God and just one of the boys, so to speak.

Absolutely! Human beings ought to relate to God as God defines the relationship. God has spoken. God has communicated. He revealed truth and the manner in which his creatures would be able to attain the destiny God prepares for them. The heavenly Father has sent his Son, Jesus, who is "the way, the truth and the life".

But there are millions of followers of Islam. They are located in great part in so called Arab speaking countries. Many countries in Asia, the Mideast, and Africa are predominantly Moslem. And many Americans profess belief in Islam.

The religion began with a man named Mohammed in 622 AD. He spent years in the Arabian city of Mecca, preaching against the many pagan idols that were honored there. He was driven out and fled to Medina, another city in Arabia. Mohammed and followers returned to Mecca in 630 AD to destroy the idols in the shrine (Kaaba). He transformed the site into a mosque, a house of worship of the one, true God. The people there came to accept Mohammed and his teachings.

Were pressures brought upon them? Strong arm tactics?

History bears witness to conquest by the sword. Holy wars were waged (jihad). Within a century caliphs, Moslem leaders and successors of Mohammed encompassed the Persian empire and a great part of the Christian Byzantine Empire. The Christian leader, Charles Martel, and his armies, halted their progress at the Battle of Tours in 732.

Today there are millions of Mohamedans in many countries. We see them kneeling in prayer on television. They have persevered in their faith. Basically what is the Moslem belief?

Mohammed claimed to have revelations from God. There is but one true God, and Mohammed is God's messenger. His followers wrote down his teachings and the revelations. This holy book is called the Koran, which means "recitation". Its content resembles the Old Testament, the Talmud, and the New Testament, stories about Jesus.

Is the Koran memorized?

Yes, and recited during prayer in the mosques. Students memorize the Koran. They make it part of themselves, drill it into their very being, so to speak. There is much in the Koran which is uplifting and inspiring. It spells out conduct and how to live.

What else do they believe in?

Heaven, hell, life is a test and a preparation for the next life, angels, last judgment, honor for parents, kindness, generosity etc.

This sounds pretty good. It should make for a better world.

The word, Islam, means "submission" in Arabic. This is a fundamental characteristic of the Moslem faith, submission to God. Surely a person who places God first in life has a true perspective. The Mohammedan's duties are summarized in these five ways: 1. a profession of faith that there is one God, Allah, and Mohammed is God's prophet; 2. prayer (five times a day facing Mecca); 3. almsgiving; 4. Fasting (during the month of Ramadan, from dawn to sunset); and 5. A pilgrimage to Mecca, at least once during one's lifetime.

It is generally known that drinking alcoholic beverages in Moslem countries is forbidden.

And there are other disciplines and details. The eating of pork is not allowed. Punishments for those caught stealing or committing adultery are usually severe.

It appears that there is influence from both Judaism and Christianity in Islam.

Mohammed lived in the 600's, the seventh century. Christianity was already established. In all probability there were both Christians and Jews living in Arabia at that time.

The history of the world can not be told without the histories of religions. They are intertwined.

This is exemplified in Jerusalem on Mount Moriah. This is where Abraham, the Father of the Jews, was about to sacrifice his son, Isaac. It is the site of the first temple, built under King Solomon's reign and completed in 960 BC. It was destroyed in 587 BC by the Babylonians. A second temple was built under King Herod in 520 BC. This was the temple visited by Jesus. This was destroyed by the Romans in 70 AD.

The Arabs conquered Palestine in 638 AD. Within fifty years the Mosque of Omar (Dome of The Rock) was constructed on Mount Moriah. This beautiful shrine of marble and mosaics is sacred to the Moslems. They trace their ancestry to Abraham, too. They say that Solomon, Elijah, David and Mohammed all prayed there. Legend says that it was from this very rock that Mohammed ascended to heaven.

And there is still another Moslem house of worship on Mount Moriah, the Aksa Mosque. Some think the structure was originally a Christian basilica in honor of Mary, Christ's mother. The Emperor Justinian built the basilica in 536 AD, and the Moslems converted the church into a mosque. And we can not forget the Crusades. From the eleventh to the thirteenth centuries there were armed Christian expeditions to recover the holy sites from the Moslem Arabs.

Are wars and violence inevitably triggered by differences in religion?

No! Religion is essentially the relationship people are to have with God. God defines the relationship. There is nothing in the teaching of Jesus that commands the use of force. However those who identify with religious systems feel at times compelled to take up arms. History bears witness to what has happened.

So this is background, leading up to what is necessary for a true relationship with God?

Yes! God communicates in time and in place. The picture will become clear.

Chapter Seven

RESPECT NOT RIVALRY

You have to admit that there is rivalry between and among religious people. For someone on the outside and looking in, this seems futile, even immature.

There is ill feeling, even hostility among religious factions. I agree that this is senseless, but it happens. This attitude hinders the relationship that someone might develop with God. "My team is better than your team." There is a need to be dispassionate, objective. A person who seeks the truth needs to pray for ideal dispositions. Truth can be elusive because of the psychological baggage we carry. Prejudice! Bias! Happy those who hear God's word in a spirit of openness. They shall bear fruit in perseverance. This advice is a paraphrase on a parable Jesus told about sowing seeds.

How should we feel about those who embrace Islam?
We should love them because God loves them.

That answer is short and direct. Easier said than done.
The Catholic Church, in its document Nostra Aetate, NA 3, (Vatican Council II), said, "The Church has a high regard for the Muslims. They worship God, who is one, living and subsistent, merciful and mighty, the Creator of heaven and earth, who has spoken to men." Pope John Paul II has met with Muslim leaders in Rome, and, on many occasions, while

visiting their countries. He said that dialogue between Catholics and Muslims is "more necessary than ever".

In another Vatican II document, Lumen Gentium, (16; NA 3) relating to relationship between the two religions, the Church says, "The plan of salvation also includes those who acknowledge the Creator, in the first place amongst whom are the Muslims; these profess to hold the faith of Abraham, and together with us they adore the one merciful God, mankind's judge on the last day."

What about the Protestants? There are many denominations. Didn't they come into existence originally protesting against the Catholic Church? There has to be some sort of rivalry.

The Protestant Reformation began in the 1500's. Today there are many divisions. These are visible in the churches that line the streets in towns and cities across the land. In St. Albans, a small city in the northern part of Vermont, there are several churches near Taylor Park. Panning with a camera from right to left, these churches come in to focus: St. Mary's Catholic Church, St. Luke's Episcopal Church, St. Paul's Methodist Church, and the First Congregational Church. A stone's throw away, the First Baptist Church, and within a short walking distance, Holy Angels Catholic Church. And there are other churches in town and close by. This scene is typical and repeated in countless other cities and towns throughout New England and the nation. The division in Christianity is set in stone, so to speak.

But, in answer to your question, yes, they came into existence protesting against the Catholic Church. This did not happen at one time. It was a movement that involved governments as well as church authorities. The splintering of Christ's Church was initiated in Germany about 1520 and extended through the 16th, 17th, 18th, 19th and the 20th centuries. Even today, new groups are forming.

What is the cause of such division among Christian churches? Does everybody want to do their own thing?

Christ prayed for unity on the night before he died. It was at the Last Supper. He foresaw the great challenge ahead for his Church. Imploring his heavenly Father for the grace his apostles would need he said, "Consecrate them in the truth. You word is truth. As you sent me into the world, so I sent them into the world. And I consecrate myself for them, so they may also be consecrated in truth." Mindful of those who would come to be Christians, Jesus prayed, "I pray not only for them, but also for those who will believe in me through their word, so that they may all be one, as you, Father, in me, and I in you, that they may also be in us, that the world may believe that you sent me." John 17:17-21

Yes, it does seem that folks want to do their own thing. They wish to interpret God's word their own way. There is a great need to see the wisdom in an authentic voice, an authority to clarify the true meaning of God's word.

Like an independent committee maybe? This sounds like talk from Washington, DC, the seat of our country's government. When there is doubt, or some suspicion that the powers to-be might not be impartial, there is a call for an independent committee.

The number of Christian divisions and/or denominations is staggering. Some years ago Rev. Dr. David B. Barrett, an Anglican clergyman, headed up a task force of researchers to produce the World Christian Encyclopedia. Their effort of fourteen years cover the time span from 30 AD to 2000. This voluminous work, (1,010 pages), attempted to categorize and count every soul. Time Magazine featured this story in its May 3, 1982 issue. The article said that Dr. Barrett concluded that the United States is a very disparate nation with 2,050 Christian and non-Christian denominations. The combined U.S. Christian population in 1982 was estimated at 161 million.

I had no idea that Christianity was so disparate. So Protestantism is more of a movement, an umbrella term, for numerous faith communities.

The article goes on to say that the largest distinct category of Protestant groups is not made up of so called mainline or traditional groups, like the Lutherans, but of evangelicals, Pentecostals, an estimated 51 million. The Our Sunday Visitor 1999 Catholic Almanac tells us that there are more than 250 Protestant church bodies in the United States.

These distinctions are overwhelming. Slow up a little. Explain how the present situation developed.

There is a caution about over-simplifying, trying to cover five centuries in a short time and in a few words. Martin Luther, an Augustinian monk and Catholic priest, registered public protest against abuses that he perceived in the Catholic Church. This was in 1517. His defiance was enhanced with some help from political powers in Germany. Other reformers followed in other European countries.

I believe I am going to have some trouble sorting this out and keeping it straight.

The history of religion, particularly Christianity, appears as a tangled web. Events are intertwined. They involve the lives of many people. Their relationship with God takes twists and turns.

Unwittingly we are all children of history. How our parents and ancestors worshipped has a lot to do with the way we worship today. They pass on their faith to their descendents. Guess we can say they pass on their lack of faith, too.

In Rainham, Essex, England, there is a public cemetery, which is called a council cemetery. The burial arrangements reflect how disparate we are. One half of the cemetery is for Church of England burials. One quarter of the cemetery is for Catholics. And the remaining quarter is for non-conformists.

What is a non-conformist?

A non-conformist was person who refused to conform to King Henry, the Eighth's 1534 Act of Supremacy. Henry, the King of England, wanted an annulment from his wife, Catherine of Aragon. Pope Clement VII denied him. So Henry declared himself free out outside authorities, including the Catholic Church. Henry raided the monasteries for their wealth. He became the head of the Church in England. Then he had Archbishop Thomas Cramner declare his marriage null. Henry went on to attempt marriage five more times. He tried to coerce his subjects in belonging to his state established church.

The plot thickens. Does this include Catholics and various Protestant groups?

Yes! England was predominantly Catholic at that time. Pope Gregory I sent Augustine and his forty monks to evangelize the country in 597. The English became mainly Catholic and loyal to the pope.

Chapter Eight

ECUMENISM

How Catholic is England today?

Less than 10 percent! According to the 1999 Our Sunday Visitor Catholic Almanac only 8.5 percent of the people are Catholic. There are between 4 and 5 million Catholics in a total population of 47.5 million inhabitants. The United Kingdom includes England, Scotland, Wales and Northern Ireland. Catholics in Wales are about 5 percent.

But the percentage of Catholics presumably was much higher before the Reformation and the reign of Henry VIII.

Christianity came to the British Isles soon after Christ's death and resurrection. According to tradition, Joseph of Arimathea journeyed there and built the first church or chapel. All four gospels, Matthew, Mark, Luke and John, mention this man, as a disciple of Jesus. He was the one who requested the body of Christ from the Roman governor, Pontius Pilate. He, and a man named Nicodemus, placed Christ's body in a garden tomb near the crucifixion site. Joseph sailed to England. There is a sign marking the spot of this ancient chapel dedicated to the Blessed Virgin Mary. The sign is found in the ruins of a 7th century abbey in Glastonbury.

In the centuries following, the Catholic Church grew. St. Augustine and his missionaries evangelized. Others came after them communicating the gospel from shore to shore.

So King Henry VIII was a faithful Catholic until Pope Clement denied him a divorce, or an annulment.

Henry received the title "Defensor Fidei", Defender of The Faith, when the Protestant movement was developing. The times were turbulent. There was great social upheaval. Henry defended the Catholic Church against these protesting Christian sects. Then, when Henry could not have his own way, he assumed the authority of the Catholic Church. He set about persecuting members of the Catholic Church and members of the non-conforming Protestant groups. Priests lost their lives.

You may remember the highly acclaimed movie, A Man For All Seasons. Thomas More, the chancellor of the country, was imprisoned in the Tower of London. He was a married man with a son and three daughters. Thomas refused to comply with Henry's Act of Supremacy. In 1535 Thomas More was beheaded. In 1935 he was officially declared a saint, canonized. He is the patron of lawyers.

How are the traditional Protestant churches different from the evangelistic Protestant churches? Apparently there is a difference.

The so-called main line Protestant churches, or traditional ones, are those started some centuries ago. They include Lutherans, Presbyterians, Baptists, Methodists and so on. In the colonial America there were members of the state established Church of England. They became Episcopalians after America's Revolutionary War.

The evangelicals are those Protestants who are quite conservative in their interpretation of the Bible. It is estimated that in the United States there are about 45 million evangelicals belonging to many different Protestant denominations. Some are characterized as fundamentalists, others as Pentecostals, and some identify themselves in both categories.

So mainstream Protestants, or traditional Protestants, differ in their approach to the Bible than evangelicals. They understand God's word differently. Would you say evangelicals interpret more fundamentally?

Generally speaking, yes. A basic tenet of Protestantism is that the Bible is the sole rule of faith. The interpretation of God's word presents a problem.

How so? If God has said something, it ought to be clear.

There is no fault to be taken with God and his communication. The challenge is to understand what God said and what God means. Underlying the Protestant approach is the individual and personal interpretation that is placed on God's word. It is easy to see that there is much difference of opinion. The multiplicity of denominations bears witness to this.

How about an example?

Was the world created in six days, as the Book of Genesis says? Is this to be interpreted literally? The fundamentalists would say, yes. Others would say that this belies science and the evolution of beings. The "six days" represents a literary form. The "six days" may mean considerably long periods of time. Shall we understand the revelation of the world's origin as described in the Bible literally or figuratively? Since God himself revealed the world's beginnings in the Bible, and since God created the world, there ought not to be discrepancy. God does not contradict himself.

When did this distinction between traditional and evangelical Protestants come about?

At the beginning of the 1900's. It is seen to be a reaction against the liberal theology and secular trends among mainstream Protestants.

Are the evangelicals the "born again" people?

The term "born again" is not new. Jesus told a man, Nicodemus, that he had to be born again. It is generally understood as mean being baptized, born again of water and of the Holy Spirit. But the current understanding among evangelicals is that a person has a grace-filled experience encountering Jesus. In some way there is an assurance of salvation.

What about the phenomenon of speaking in tongues, prophecies, healings etc.?

These are associated with the Pentecostals. The Assemblies of God are Pentecostals. Their members number about two million in the United

States. They are strongly fundamental in their practice and adherence to the Bible.

It seems that, since the Reformation in the 1500's, there has been increasing division among Christians. Denominations have proliferated. Is there any hope of Christian unity?

Humanly speaking, probably not. Like Humpty-Dumpty, all the king's horses and all the king's men could not put him together again. However, with God, nothing is impossible.

Is anybody working on this? Has there been any kind of progress?

The ecumenical movement exists. The word, ecumenical, comes from the Greek, "oikoumenikos" meaning "of or from the whole world". That's the size of the challenge, worldwide. Catholics and other Christians pray together during the Week of Prayer for Christian Unity, January 18-25. There are theological gatherings and studies. Joint efforts in charitable works are fostered, mutual collaboration. It is probably safe to say that there is greater understanding.

There has been progress, but there is still a long way to go.

The Catholic Church's Vatican Council II in 1964 addressed the challenge of Christian unity with its document "Unitatis Redintegratio", "the restoration of unity". This is a principal concern. In 1993 priorities were expressed in a Directory of Application of Principles and Norms on Ecumenism. Common elements of faith were articulated. Guidelines emphasizing truth and fairness in mutual relations, sensitivity; the need for dialogue; common prayer; and faithfulness to Christ. Catholics are encouraged to seek Christian perfection personally, to be renewed and purified in soul.

Should everyone worship together?

Pray together, on occasion. There are specific guidelines. The Catholic Church has a prohibition of Catholics worshipping in official Protestant liturgies.

Chapter Nine

WORSHIP

Why the prohibition?

Full participation of Catholics in Protestant liturgies implies profession of the faith expressed in the liturgy. Intercommunion by Catholics in Protestant liturgies is also not allowed. There are serious differences in belief. There is also a profound difference in the manner of worship. There is not a meeting of minds or hearts. Catholics and Protestants differ in their appreciation of Jesus Christ and his teachings.

Are we trivializing now? Nit picking? You say that on occasion Catholics and Protestants may pray together, but not worship together.

There was a time when some, impatient to get on with Christian unity, said, in effect, "Let's pray and sing and worship together and not worry about the dogmas." It is unwise to dismiss official teachings. This may just lead to further confusion, and even a greater splintering of Christianity. It is important to be faithful to God as God defines the relationship we are to have with him.

What is the difference between prayer and worship?

Prayer is talking with God. There are no office hours. Day and night we are free to speak with God, who hears every word. Everyone should pray. Jesus taught us how to pray by giving us the Lord's Prayer, the Our Father. Say the words and you approach the heavenly Father in the best

possible way. Dispositions of mind and heart, of course, should be in conformity with the heavenly Father's will.

When we speak to God usually we ask, we praise, we express sorrow for sinning, and we thank the good Lord, who is the giver of all our gifts.

Don't we do this when we worship? Seems to me there is petition and contrition in Sunday services. Praise and thanks, too. We lift our voices in songs that express all these sentiments.

Yes, and this is very good. The manner in which Protestants and Catholics worship is very different. Both Protestants and Catholics pray and proclaim the scriptures, that is, Bible selections are read. There are sermons or homilies. Churches are alive with the sound of music. The profound difference lies in the priesthood.

Catholics have a validly ordained priesthood. The priests are empowered to change the bread and wide into the Body and Blood of Christ. Jesus Christ acts through them , changing the substance of bread and wine into himself. Through them, Christ offers himself at the altar during Mass.

So in Catholic theology, it is Christ who offers himself. Is this worship?

Yes! Jesus offered himself to the heavenly Father on the night before he died. It was at the Last Supper, the Passover meal. He changed the bread and wine into himself. He empowered his apostles as priests, "Do this in remembrance of me." Then, the next day, he offered himself on the cross. Christ bowed down, worshipped, made a total offering, suffering death itself.

Is that what worship is? A total offering?

Bowing down before the Lord, acknowledging God as the Supreme Being, is worship. It is adoration. Catholics unite with Christ in worship. They offer themselves with him in his magnanimous gesture. They are one in mind and heart with Christ. There is no other higher form of praise.

Explain the priesthood a little more? Catholic priests are different than ministers, although they lead their parishioners in prayer. Both preach and baptize and counsel.

Many of the Protestant denominations do not claim a priesthood in their communities of faith. The Anglicans, that is, the ordained of the Church of England and the Episcopalians, do claim a priesthood. However, there was an official pronouncement by Pope Leo XIII in 1896 against the validity of their priestly orders or ordinations. He cited a break in the apostolic succession by Matthew Parker when Parker was head of the Anglican hierarchy in 1559. Apostolic succession means an unbroken line from the time of Christ's apostles through the ordination of Catholic bishops and priests.

Well, what makes a priest, a priest?

He is a man, chosen from among men, to offer sacrifice. There were Old Testament priests. They were of the tribe of Levi. They offered lambs and oxen and goats and doves in the Temple in Jerusalem. Their rituals and offerings were specified in the Mosaic Law. The element of sacrifice has to be understood and appreciated. Things were offered in worship, in sacrifice. Priests were anointed, officially designated, to sacrifice these victims. This was to acknowledge God by offering these things which were precious.

But the magnificent temple in Jerusalem no longer exists. There are no more animal offerings.

Correct! The temple was torn down in the year 70 AD by the Romans. There are no more burnt offerings, nor animal sacrifices, among the Jews.

Has the priesthood changed?

Yes! The priesthood was brought to perfection by Jesus Christ.

What does that mean?

All the sacrifices of the Old Testament were done away with. Through the dynamic of Christ's own sacrifice and his priesthood, the relationship to and with the heavenly Father was profoundly changed. Jesus is the one and only priest. The name "Christ" means the anointed one. He offered himself. He is both the victim and the priest who offers. The bulls and oxen and lambs and goats could not of themselves restore a loving

relationship with God. They were insufficient, incapable. They were not able to expiate the sins of the world from the beginning of time.

So Christ is a priest?

Yes! He is, in a sense, the one and only priest. The ordained priests share in Christ's priesthood. Christ speaks through them. At the Eucharist, the Mass, they say, "This is my Body! This is the cup of my Blood…". Baptized parishioners also share in Christ's priesthood, but in a different way. This is called the priesthood of the laity. They share in Christ's mission. They are not empowered to transubstantiate the bread and wine into Christ himself, his Body and Blood. But they are in harmony with the ordained priest as he celebrates Mass.

So worship in the Catholic Mass has this difference and profound dimension as compared to Protestant liturgical worship. But the Protestants do have communion services.

Protestant communion services are memorials. Transubstantiation does not take place.

Catholics, then, believe that Jesus Christ is truly present in the Eucharist, rather than just a memorial.

That's correct. The Mass is a memorial insomuch as the death and resurrection of Christ are commemorated. But it is more than that. Christ actually offers himself at the altar. This is his Holy Sacrifice. He died once and for all on the cross, but he continues to offer himself in the unbloody manner in the Eucharist.

Has this always been true even from the beginning of the Church?

Yes! From the beginning, from the Last Supper, all through the ages to this present day. God's work of salvation is on-going.

Are there references in the Bible that support this belief?

Yes! Clearly in sacred scripture and in the constant tradition of the Church!

Chapter Ten

UNION WITH CHRIST

Is the Bible the sole rule of faith? Does it contain all the answers to a proper relationship with God?

The Bible is wonderful. It is the word of God. When God speaks, everyone ought to listen. Sincere people are inspired and guided by God's holy word. But it is not the only source of God's communication. There is also tradition, that is, the official way Christians have believed and acted in the Church. A line in the Bible reads, "Now Jesus did many other signs in the presence of [his] disciples that are not written in this book." (John 20:30) St. John, who wrote his gospel later than Matthew, Mark and Luke, probably about 90AD, was a special friend of Jesus and an eyewitness to the miracles that Jesus performed.

But many teachings can be shown or proven through the Bible. Right?

Of course! When students for the priesthood pursue their studies in seminaries, they go step by step though the basic teachings of Christ. A thesis is carefully and methodically set forth with proofs from sacred scripture, tradition, and reason. It is good to remember that the Bible was not complete when Christ established his Church. There were books to be written. The 27 books in the New Testament were not completed for many years. Yet Christians believed in Christ, followed Christ, and even, died for Christ before the completion of the Bible.

So the early Church grew without the Bible?

Christ did not say to his apostles, "Okay, men, sit down and write everything I say and do." He did say is, "Go, therefore, and make disciples of all nations, baptizing them in the name of the Father, and of the Son, and of the holy Spirit, teaching them to observe all that I have commanded you. And behold, I am with you always, until the end of the age." (Matthew 28:19-20) The apostles communicated. They preached and informed. They prayed. They gave personal witness to Jesus Christ. It was only after 30, 40, 50 and more years, that they penned the contents of the Bible.

Is it written anywhere in the Bible that the Bible itself is the sole rule of faith?
No! There is no such statement. This is not to belittle the Bible, nor the very fine people who read the Bible reverently. The source of belief and God's teachings are both in the Bible and in sacred tradition. Jesus is with his Church. He acts through the authority he instilled into the Church. Christ's Church is a living body. He did say, "I am with you all days...".

What are those quotations that indicate that Jesus is truly a priest?
Speaking of Jesus, St. Paul, in his letter to the Hebrews says, "Surely he did not help angels but rather the descendents of Abraham; therefore he had to become like his brothers in every way, that he might be a merciful and faithful high priest before God to expiate the sins of people." (Hebrews 2: 16-17) The very idea of sacrifice indicates atonement for wrongs. It is an offering to God who has been offended
In that same letter, Paul declares, "Therefore, since we have a great high priest who has passed through the heavens, Jesus, the Son of God, let us hold fast to our confession. For we do not have a high priest who is unable to sympathize with our weaknesses, but one who has been similarly tested in every way, yet without sin." (Hebrews 4:14)

Now you also said that Jesus is present in the Eucharist, under the forms of bread and wine. The priest, who celebrates the Mass, acts in the person of Christ. What are some quotes that indicate Christ's true presence?
Christ promised his true presence in the Eucharist shortly after he performed the great miracle of multiplying the loaves and fishes. You

probably heard that Jesus prayed over five barley loaves and a couple fish. His disciples distributed the food to five thousand who had assembled on a hillside. There were 12 baskets of fragments left over. After they had been fed, and presumably impressed, Jesus said, "I am the living bread that came down from heaven; whoever eats this bread will live forever; and the bread that I will give is my flesh for the life of the world." (John 6:51) This was his promise.

When did he fulfill his promise?
On the night before he was crucified. It was in an upper room on Jerusalem's Mount Zion. At the Last Supper, the Passover meal, Christ instituted the Eucharist. "While they were eating, Jesus took bread, said the blessing, broke it and giving it to his disciples said, 'Take and eat; this is my body.' Then he took a cup, gave thanks, and gave it to them saying, "Drink from it all of you, for this is my blood of the covenant, which shall be shed on behalf of many for the forgiveness of sins' ". Matthew 26:26-28

Was Jesus speaking literally? Could there be any mistake in interpretation?
There is no mistake. While still on the hillside, after feeding the thousands, St. John tells us in his gospel: "The Jews quarreled among themselves, saying, "How can this man give us his flesh to eat?" Jesus said to them, "Amen, amen, I say to you, unless you eat the flesh of the Son of Man and drink his blood, you do not have life within you.'" (John 6:52-53) Some walked away. But Christ did not change his teaching.

Are there other supportive quotations?
St. Paul is quite clear in his letter to the Corinthians. "The cup of blessing that we bless, is it not a participation in the blood of Christ ? The bread that we break, is it not a participation of the body of Christ? (1 Corinthians 10:16) St. Paul also says, "Whoever eats the bread or drinks the cup of the Lord unworthily will have to answer for the body and blood of the Lord...Anyone who eats and drinks without discerning the body, eats and drinks judgment on himself." (1 Corinthians 11:27,29)

So, at the Mass, Communion is truly a holy communion with Christ. Are Catholics emotional about this? To be one with God, with Jesus, who is both God and man, is awesome.

It is possible for some people to be emotional, but generally speaking, communicants are not. They believe and they profess their belief. When the priest gives them Holy Communion he says, "The Body of Christ", and they reply," Amen". Somehow God shields us from his magnificence. There was a feeling among the Jews, and a saying as well, that no one sees the face of God and lives. Holy Communion is, indeed, an unspeakable privilege.

In the Church's document on Social Communication, a pastoral instruction, there is a line, powerful and expressive. "In the institution of the Holy Eucharist, Christ gave us the most perfect, the most intimate form of communion between God and man possible in this life, and out of this, the deepest possible unity between men." (#11)

What did St. Paul mean when he spoke of receiving the bread and cup of the Lord unworthily?

A person should not approach the altar for Holy Communion unless they are free of serious sins. Communicants are to be in love with God, in harmony with God, not having offended in a serious manner. True sorrow, contrition and confession are to take place before uniting with Jesus Christ in the Eucharist. Those with unconfessed mortal sins must seek Christ's pardon in the Sacrament of Reconciliation. To receive Holy Communion unworthily is sacrilegious.

Are there many Catholics who refrain from Communion because of serious sins?

This is difficult to say. Who knows besides God and the individual? But there is incentive for a better life. A person of faith wants to be one with God. Small sins, what they call venial sins, do not break one's friendship with God. Sincere participants express their sorrow in prayer before Holy Communion. This wonderful sacrament, the Eucharist, is said to be both the sign and the cause a Christian's unity with God.

So Protestants are not permitted to receive Holy Communion in the Catholic Church. Right?

Chapter Eleven

THE HUMAN CONDITION

That is correct. We do have hope that one day there will be genuine Christian unity. One flock and one Shepherd, Jesus Christ!

Do you hope that all Christians will receive Christ in Holy Communion?
Hope and pray! There has to be a real eagerness, a yearning, to be one with Christ.

I don't see a great deal of evidence of this enthusiasm. Have I missed something?
There is sincere interest among many people, both Catholic and Protestant. Pope John Paul II surely has been instrumental in furthering the cause of ecumenism. Some Protestant leaders, too. Among the rank and file? There does not appear to be a lot of activity. After Vatican Council II in the early 1960's there were small study groups that focused on the challenge.

And now? Interest has waned?
There is a general observation about church-goers and relationship with God. When economic times are favorable, when there are jobs, when food is plentiful, a percentage of people become comfortable. Almost as if they did not need to pray and to worship. Almost as if they did not need God. During the Depression, in the 1930's, here in the United States,

times were tough. Parishioners in desperate conditions packed churches making novenas.

What has this to do with ecumenism and the quest for Christian unity?

This is an observation about people, their outlook, their attitude, and their on-going relationship with God. How they relate to God overlaps in their relationships with each other.

This is an editorial on the human condition.

There is a need to see things God's way. What does God want? If we focus inwardly, we limit our horizons.

Indifference and apathy plays a part when it comes to Christian unity?

Some indifference and apathy! "I've got mine. You get yours." "I've got enough to do to think about my soul. You take care of your own." There is a ripple effect flowing through the ages which, believe it or not, is a consequence of original sin.

Blame it on Adam and Eve!

We are responsible for our own actions. But there are inherited weaknesses. God makes allowances for our human frailty. We are free. Nevertheless, we are accountable. We must be honest with ourselves and with God. In particular circumstances it may take time and patience to sort things out.

For example?

A woman came to a priest for instructions in the Catholic faith. She was faithful to weekly classes and attended Mass regularly on Sundays. When her course was completed, she indicated that there was nothing she did not understand. She believed in the teachings of Christ and his Church.

But what?

Her father was an older man, not in good health, and had a bad heart condition. He had strong feelings about the Catholic Church. She felt that, if she became a Catholic, it would be inviting trouble She feared for her father's reaction. She delayed her entry into the Church.

That's certainly being human. Perhaps prudent, too.

There was another young woman, a Protestant, engaged to a Catholic. She requested religious instructions, not because she intended to convert, but that she might understand her husband-to-be and his religion. The priest began by telling her about the most beautiful feature of the Catholic faith, the true presence of Christ in the Eucharist. She continued weekly instructions. One evening she told the good Father that she had decided to become a Catholic. There was some hesitancy, however. Some fear. She was active in her own church and sang in the choir. He parents were devout in their parish participation. She was uneasy, not knowing how her mother and father would react to her conversion.

This is very understandable. Very human, to say the least.

The priest advised her to continue praying, to be married in the Catholic Church, as was her intention. He thought it wise for her to remain Protestant. After she was married for a time, living with her husband, and maturing in confidence, then, she might ask to become a Catholic. After a year of marriage, she returned to the priest and said she was ready. Her sensitivity to her parents and her love for them was not diminished. But the intense preparations for marriage, the details and anticipation for this milestone in her life was past. Now she was confident and comfortable with her decision to follow Christ in the Church.

Nice story! Presumable they lived happily ever after. What about anti-Catholic and anti-Protestant feelings? Such antipathy does exist.

True! And this has to be confronted in a person's mind and heart. Jesus, of course, has the perfect solution, practical, but demanding. He says we are to love our enemies, do good to those who hate us, and always return good for evil. This is the only way to break the vicious cycle of accusation and recrimination, constant bickering and ill-feeling.

It is difficult to separate our emotions from the thought process. In the heat of an argument someone might snap, "I don't care what you say. I would not agree with you if this was the end of the world and you where the last person alive."

There was a Catholic, an older lady of Irish descent, who would read the obituaries in the daily paper. If no Catholics were listed, she would remark, "No one's dead!"

She evidently had strong feelings.

Deep seated sentiments go back years, even centuries. During the 1800's, during the famine in Ireland, more than a million died. The Irish were staunchly Catholic. There was enticement, pressure, by the British to have them change their faith, become Protestant, members of the Church of England. Soup was given to those who complied. They were called "soupers". Certainly not a term of endearment.

Hostility and resentment continues in Northern Ireland to this day. It is not all because of religion. Civil rights are involved. We can only pray that peace will enter the hearts of all Catholic and Protestants in that land which has suffered so dearly.

And prejudice and bias exists in the United States, too. Any examples?

There has been progress. We are still searching for a perfect world and ideal dispositions. A person' heart has to be in the right place.

Some years ago there used to be signs: "Catholics need not apply". When jobs are scarce, and when folks have to eat, they are tempted to conceal their religious convictions. One woman tells the story of a friend who was about to apply for a job. She posed the question: "What if they ask you if you are Catholic?" Her friend replied, "I'll tell them that I am not."

She was prepared to deny her religious affiliation.

Jesus is clear about a person's convictions and loyalty to him. "Everyone who acknowledges me before others, I will acknowledge before my heavenly Father. But whoever denies me before others, I will deny before my heavenly Father." (Matthew 10:32-33) Jesus predicted that his followers would be persecuted. He said that those who did not take up their crosses and follow him, could not be his disciples. God has consideration for our humanity, but at the same time, our loyalty must be unswerving.

Today we continue to be challenged among the many Christians and the many denominations.

Chapter Twelve

OUR BROTHERS AND SISTERS

There are so many of us in this part of the world who are separated and divided from one another because of religion. Cities, towns and villages have folks who are related to one another, but disagree on the way to go to God.

Christian disunity is a way of life, a culture. Many are indifferent to this because they are not overly concerned about religion in the first place. They settle into complacency, saying, in effect, it does not bother me one way or another.

But when a Protestant falls in love with a Catholic, or vice versa, religious differences are magnified. If there is a mixed marriage, decisions must be made about the children's faith and practice. If one is a convinced Christian and the other is hardly interested, it is challenging, if not impossible, for husband and wife to have a genuine meeting of minds.

Husbands and wives take vows, make sacred promises, to be married to each other with God as their witness. It is God who joins them together in matrimony. They are no longer two, but one, as Christ teaches in the gospels. They are challenged to develop and to sustain a bond of love. Their union is physical and psychological. They are to be soul-mates. Like all human relationships, compromises are needed in marriage. But when it comes to God's will, which is perfect truth, there can be no essential compromises.

What does the Catholic Church do to assist couples in preparation for marriage, especially if they profess faiths different from one another?

All dioceses have premarital instructions, often called, Pre-Cana Conferences. There are five basic adjustments for couples to make when they marry: personal, domestic, sexual, social and economic. The courses include information about the sacredness of marriage. Baptized couples receive a sacrament when they marry. Additional information about the basic teachings of Jesus and his Church are provided for a non-Catholic. The instructions are not an attempt to convert the non-Catholic party, but try to assist the person in greater understanding.

When family members belong to difference religions, Catholic and/or non-Catholic, is there an extra burden. Does this divide them?

It may divide them. Jesus had something to say about this. He proclaimed the Kingdom of God. There is often a purifying process, leaving an old life and beginning a new life. Conversion demands change. Christ's message could meet with acceptance or rejection. He indicated that this could be a source of conflict and dissension. "From now on a household of five will be divided three against two and two against three; a father will be divided against his son and a son against his father, a mother against her daughter and a daughter against her mother, a mother-in-law against her daughter-in-law and a daughter-in-law against her mother-in-law." (Luke 12:52-53)

It seems strange that Christ or his teachings should divide people. It is incongruous and out of character.

Jesus has no intention to set people at odds with one another. He teaches love for God and love for our neighbors. Love is for everyone.

But apparently, division happens.

Unwittingly, it happens! If everyone in the entire world loved one another, this would be a perfect world.

Catholics should love Protestants, and Protestants should love Catholics.

And Catholics and Protestants should love Jews, and Muslims, and Hindus...and everyone.

How come it doesn't work out?

There is nothing to prevent people from loving one another. Love is centered in the will. Love is the intent to do good to others. It is in the giving and not in the getting. When it comes to loving God, we must embrace his holy will. If you love me, keep my commandments. Obedience surely goes with love. We try to please God by conforming to his wishes. The difficulty lies in the dedication to do God's will. It lies in the understanding of what God wishes. Those with other religions presumably are convinced that they should go in other directions.

What do Catholics and Protestants have in common?

The Decree on Ecumenism promulgated during Vatican Council II cites several elements that Catholic and Protestants enjoy: among them, the Bible, God's written word, a life of grace, faith, hope and charity, gifts of the Holy Spirit. Although there are many Protestant denominations, and many members within them, there are millions of believers who have a genuine love for Jesus. They read the scriptures. They appreciate Christ's teachings. They are motivated. They have a spirit about them which is sincere and Christ-like. Countless numbers of Catholics and Protestants have a mutual love and respect for one another.

What about points of disagreement?

Well, sorry to say, there is not complete agreement. The Vatican II document mentions: confession of Christ as Lord, Christ as Mediator between God and man, the Trinity, difference in reverence for scripture as the revealed word of God, Baptism, the Lord's Supper, Christian life and worship, faith in action, and certain moral questions.

That list is a tall order. There are fundamental differences. Does the multiplicity of Protestant denominations itself compound the situation? Does it complicate the ultimate solution?

It doesn't help. It would be greatly beneficial to be united and be able to present solidarity in faith to non-Christians. I am certain that many people see this disunity a stumbling block and a barrier to sharing the faith with others. It makes evangelization, the essential mission of Christ's Church, even more challenging.

Give me an example of a moral question that contributes to this divisiveness.

Abortion! The Catholic Church is absolutely unswerving in its pro-life position. The National Council of Catholic Bishops has an annual program called Respect Life. The Church's teaching is that God has absolute dominion over human life from conception to natural death. It is incontrovertible that human life begins at conception. God initiates life. Those who terminate human life sin seriously. One of the laws in the Church's Code of Canons says abortion is not only a serious sin, but also a crime. Catholics who knowingly and intentionally commit abortions incur excommunication.

And there are Protestant denominations that permit abortion?

Some denominations are pro-life, others consider abortion permissible under certain circumstances. It is unfortunate that there is not a united stand among Christians.

And, I suppose, there other disagreements on moral matters.

Among them divorce and remarriage, homosexual unions, and the list grows.

The Catholic Church manifests a strong authority. It is not hesitant in declaring it position, even in controversial matters.

At a local clergy breakfast, priests and ministers chatted about things religious and whatnot. A question surfaced. A priest expressed the clear teaching of the Church. A minister near him said, "I wish we had some one like the Pope." After all the discussion and research is completed, there is a bottom line. The clergyman was not being disloyal to his denomination, but acknowledged the advantage of authoritative declaration.

The Catholic Church is not a democracy.

Jesus did not establish his Church as a democracy. He centered his authority in St. Peter, the first Pope, and in Peter's successors. Each bishop has authority in his territory, in his diocese, subject to the Holy Father. In his infinite wisdom Christ fashioned his family of faith in the best possible manner.

Chapter Thirteen

THE FULLNESS OF CHRIST

Is the Pope infallible?

God guides his Church, guarding it from error. This is accomplished through the authority established within the Church by Christ, and particularly in the person of the Pope. Yes! The Holy Father is infallible when he declares Christ's teachings in faith and in morals. His declarations are infallible when they are made officially, and made for the entire Church worldwide. These declarations are what they call "ex cathedra", from the throne of St. Peter, so to speak. In these cases, the Pope is not speaking privately, or just to a particular group of people.

Some people would say that this makes the Pope almost like a god.

Well, he is not a god, and the Pope himself would be the first person to disclaim this exaggeration. Notice that infallibility is only exercised when the Holy Father addresses matters relating to belief, that is, faith, and only to matters relating to practice, that is, morality. Don't ask him about futurables in the stock market because he will just laugh. He does not make predictions about the outcome of the World Series. His extraordinary power of infallibility is, in effect, Christ guiding his Church, in its relationship with the heavenly Father.

Has the Pope been infallible since the beginning of the Church?

Yes! The power is invested in St. Peter and his successors. And they have exercised this right to teach through the centuries. However, usually the Popes do not act independently or without collaboration, although the power is vested in them individually and personally.

How does the Pope collaborate?

Ordinarily he calls a meeting, or a council. There were 2860 Catholic bishops from around the world that gathered in Rome for the Second Vatican Council in the early 1960's. There have been 21 ecumenical councils in the history of the Church.

Only 21 councils?

There have been countless meetings, or synods, or councils through the centuries. An ecumenical council brings together a representation of the Church from the four corners of the world. These councils focus matters that affect all the faithful.

Do the participants vote to establish the Catholic Church's official teachings?

The bishops discuss, dialogue, debate and research. They are assisted by experts in theology. Eventually they vote on a matter. But their vote does not constitute an official teaching. The Holy Father has the last word. The process is collegial, but the final decision rests in the Pope. That's where the infallibility comes in.

What were all the councils about?

Disputes arise. Questions surface. Perhaps someone teaches in error and this leads others into error. What the Church does is clarify Christ's teaching. No one should be misdirected in their journey of faith. There have been heretical and schismatic movements.

How about some examples?

The Council of Nicaea in 325 condemned the heresy of Arianism. The Council Fathers clarified teaching about the divinity of Jesus Christ.

The Council of Trent from 1545 to 1563 defined many doctrines, principally related to the Protestant Reformation. Among its definitions: the Canon of the Bible (officially recognized books), the seven sacraments, the sacrificial nature of the Mass, the rule of faith and more. This is considered the counter-reformation council. There were so many departures from the traditional teaching of the Church by the various reformers.

Has a Pope ever made a dogmatic definition "ex cathedra" outside of an ecumenical council?

On November 1, 1950 Pope Pius XII defined the dogma of Mary's Assumption. The belief that Christ's mother, Mary, being taken to heaven bodily, was not new. The feast has been observed for centuries. There is a local tradition in Jerusalem which details the end of her life on earth. The Holy Father wanted to highlight this long standing Catholic belief with his "ex cathedra" definition. 1950 was a year dedicated to Mary, a Marian Year.

Ecumenical or general councils have take place over two millennia. All the decisions flowing from the councils are not "ex cathedra" are they?

Only those definitions specifically singled out and approved as "ex cathedra" fall under the Holy Father's infallibility. It is good to understand that the Church is teaching constantly through its bishops. The challenge is on-going to clarify Christ's teachings. Those who are baptized are blessed in the guidance they receive from Christ in his Church. It is also good to understand the Church is not inventing new doctrines. Those truths which are officially defined are already contained either in scripture or in tradition.

What was Vatican Council II all about? This is the most recent ecumenical council. Right?

Vatican II was convened by Pope John XXIII in 1963 who was looking for an "aggiornamento", an updating of the Church in modern times. The image portrayed was the Holy Father opening a window and letting the fresh air in. Pope John died before the council could finish its work. Pope Paul VI reconvened it. The council continued until 1965.

Were there any "ex cathedra" definitions about faith or morality in this council?

No! But there were 16 documents issued by Vatican II and approved by the Pope. Faith is expressed in time and in place. Conditions around the world change constantly. There are technological advancements.

Countries and peoples relate to one another differently as time goes by. The 20th century witnessed tremendous development in the fields of radio, television, film, computers and so on. Human nature does not change, but our culture, our common way of life does change.

What is the focus of the documents?

Documents are teachings. Among those promulgated by Vatican II are: worship or liturgy; the modern means of communication; the pastoral role of bishops; Christian education; missionary activity and so on. The Church, through its bishops and the Pope, addressed the role of the laity, the life of priests, and the relations of the Church to non-Christian religions.

One of the changes that stands out and affects the lives of Catholics is the change of language at Mass. Mass was celebrated in Latin for centuries. Today, the language of the Eucharistic liturgy is in the vernacular for each country.

Did the Vatican Council bring about a greater understanding of the Church itself. Do people enjoy a greater insight into the mission and activities of the Church? Has it helped the cause of ecumenism?

The Decree on Ecumenism, Unitatis Redintegratio, highlighted a principal concern. Vatican II documents serve to improve the climate of human relationships and enhance cordial relationships. And the Church demonstrates its spiritual leadership. Positions on religious matters are made clear.

"For it is through Christ's Catholic Church alone, which is the universal help toward salvation, that the fullness of the means of salvation can be obtained. It was to the apostolic college alone, of which Peter is the head, that we believe that our Lord entrusted all the blessings of the New Covenant, in order to establish on earth the one body of Christ in which all those should be fully incorporated who belong in any way to the people of God." (#3) To express it simply, the fullness of Christ is found in the Catholic Church. Jesus is "the way, the truth and the life" as he said of himself. Our way to the heavenly Father is through his Son. Christ longs for unity. This is Christ's prayer and the prayer of his Church.

Chapter Fourteen

SAINTS

What is meant by "the fullness of the means of salvation"?
This means whatever it takes to attain eternal life! What is needed for a person to reach his ultimate destiny? God wishes every person to be with him forever. But God does not compel anyone. People must freely comply with God's will. Jesus provides the means to the end.

So the Catholic Church alone has all the means for salvation. This sounds exclusive. Does this imply the rest of the world is going to hell?
Not at all! No one is saying that. Judgment belongs to God. We do not know who fails to cooperate with the grace of God. There is no list of those in hell. But there is a hell. The Bible refers to hell in various ways: "everlasting fire", "everlasting punishment", "a place of torments", and so on. Hell is to be without God for eternity.
After original sin, the sin of Adam and Eve, God was not accessible for eternity. The gates of heaven were closed, so to speak. After centuries of waiting, God intervened. The Father sent his Son, Jesus Christ. Jesus expresses this succinctly. "I am the way, and the truth and the life. No one comes to the Father except through me." (John 14:6)

But why does the Vatican II document insist that the Church alone has all the means for salvation?

Because there are so many other non-Catholic Christian denominations, some entertaining some of the teachings of Christ, but not all the teachings, not all the means of grace.

Give me some examples.
The Catholic Church has a valid priesthood. Christ is truly present in the Eucharist. Christ's authority is vested in the Catholic Church to determine what books in the Bible are authentic. Christ's living voice expresses itself in the proper interpretation of God word in the Bible. There are seven sacraments established by Christ. Many Protestant denominations differ from each other in the number of the sacraments they profess. So some non-Catholic denominations may entertain some of these teachings, but not all of them entertain all of them.

This could be quite a job sorting them all out.
Recall Christ's words when he commissioned his apostles to evangelize. "Go, therefore, and make disciples of all nations, baptizing them in the name of the Father, and of the Son, and of the holy Spirit, teaching them to observe all that I have commanded you." (Matthew 28:19-20) This is a total package, "all that I have commanded you". The fullness of the means for salvation is really the fullness of Christ.

Well then, are all non-Catholics handicapped?
It is possible for everyone on the face of the earth to be saved for eternity. Each person must cooperate with the grace of God. And God provides his grace to each person wherever they may be. He or she has to have the equivalent of Baptism of Desire. This is not an easy matter. People do not waltz into heaven. The challenge of a lifetime is not to be underestimated.

I presume you are saying chances are better if the means of salvation are more readily available.
If you were building a house and only had a hammer and a saw, it would be much more difficult than if you had a full set of carpenter's tools and a team of construction workers. A doctor might perform an emergency operation with only a pen knife. But chances are much better

if the procedure take place in a modern, fully accredited hospital. Tools and instruments do not guarantee success, but they facilitate the process.

Often people say things like, "Grandma died and went to heaven". Is this presumption?

It is a lovely thought. We do well to think highly of our good living family members and friends. But, outside of the canonized saints, we simply do not know that those who pass away are with God. Jesus once said that it was more difficult for a rich man to enter the kingdom of God than for a camel to pass through the eye of a needle. "Not everyone who says to me, 'Lord, Lord', will enter the kingdom of heaven, but only the one who does the will of my Father in heaven." (Matthew 7:21) Wishful thinking is insufficient.

What does it take to be a saint?

Heroic virtue! Loving God with our whole heart and soul! This love for God overflows into loving our family, friends, neighbors…the whole world. This is the challenge of a lifetime and a lifetime of challenge. The saints managed to become the best they could be with the grace of God.

Does God demand perfection?

God does not tolerate mediocrity. In the Book of Revelation it is written, "I know your works; I know that you are neither cold nor hot. I wish you were either cold or hot. So, because you are lukewarm, neither hot nor cold, I will spit you out of my mouth." (Revelation 3:15-16) Mediocre is untenable. Saints are totally dedicated.

At times people joke about not being saints. They say, "Oh, I'm no saint". There even seems to be bravado on occasion about being naughty. There are clever signs indicating that everything I like is illegal, immoral and fattening. Or "Look at these chocolate covered cherries! They are absolutely sinful." Is this a wrong slant on sanctity?

We do kid around at times. But no one should be proud of thwarting God's plan for eternal life. St. Paul has an interesting answer. "Do not conform yourselves to this age but be transformed by the renewal of your mind, that you may discern what is the will of God, what is good and pleasing and perfect." (Romans 12:2)

Is perfection a sine qua non condition? Does anyone enter the presence of God without perfection?

Jesus said, "So be perfect, just as your heavenly Father is perfect." (Matthew 5:48) He also instructed a rich young man who asked specifically about eternal life. Christ told him that God's commandments had to be obeyed. When the fellow replied that he was faithful to the commandments, Jesus said, "If you wish to be perfect, go, sell what you have and give to [the] poor, and you will have treasure in heaven. Then come, and follow me." (Matthew 19:21) Unfortunately the young man was attached to his wealth, So, he walked away,

Surely everyone is not called to be a monk or a nun. Ordinary persons, the people in the pews, are not obliged to take the vow of poverty.

That's true. But they are called to stewardship of the goods of this world. To be overly possessive about material things is untenable. How are we to use our blessings? Many people are blind to the millions of men, women and children trapped in the poverty of Third World countries. St. John has this admonition. "If someone who has worldly means sees a brother in need and refuses him compassion, how can the love of God remain in him? Children, let us love not in word or speech but in deed and truth." (1 John 3:17-18)

How do people become a saints?
They follow Christ and his teachings.

Can everyone become a saint?
Yes! Saints are from all walks of life. Kings and queens have become saints. St. Francis of Assisi literally lived his vow of poverty and begged from door to door. St. Theresa, the Little Flower, was a gentle nun. St. Joseph was a carpenter. St. Jerome translated the scriptures from Hebrew and Greek into Latin, the language of his day. Mary was a housewife and a mother. We are to do ordinary things well and for the glory of God. Holiness is an unconditional state needed in order to live with God for eternity.

Chapter Fifteen

REPENT AND BELIEVE

How does a person learn about Jesus Christ?
Are you interested? Would you like to become a follower?

Interested? Yes! Curious! Intrigued!
Let me guess! You would like to become a saint.

Well, that sounds a bit pretentious. Still, the way you have explained it, the alternative is not much of an option.
Nobody is going anywhere without holiness, and holiness is attained through Jesus Christ.

That's a succinct way of putting it. It seems like a good idea to check out Jesus' credentials.
To begin, pray to God. Ask for enlightenment, the ability to understand, the willingness to accept even though you may have to adjust. Becoming a follower involves more than acquiring information. Remember that there were people who met Jesus face to face and declined to become Christian.

So there is a possibility that I might study, but not be converted.
Jesus once sent his disciples on a mission. They were to go from town to town, from village to village, announcing the kingdom of God. He anticipated some opposition, some rejection. "Whoever will not receive

you or listen to your words --- go outside that house or town and shake the dust from your feet." (Matthew 10:14) God's words have to be received in receptive hearts.

Did Christ require repentance?

Yes! John, the Baptizer, whose job was to prepare people for the coming of Christ, preached repentance along the Jordan River. "Repent, for the kingdom of heaven is at hand." (Matthew 3:2) At the beginning of Christ's public ministry, he, too, emphasized the need to repent. "After John had been arrested, Jesus came to Galilee proclaiming the gospel of God. This is the time of fulfillment. The kingdom of God is at hand. Repent, and believe in the gospel." (Mark 1:14-15)

After Christ's resurrection from the dead, his apostles preached in the same way. "Peter [said] to them, 'Repent, and be baptized, every one of you, in the name of Jesus Christ for the forgiveness of your sins; and you will receive the gift of the holy Spirit." (Acts 2:38)

What if I feel that I do not have a lot to repent? Most people live ordinary lives. They do not get into trouble.

Everyone has a need to repent. Everyone has an on-going need for personal renewal. Everyone is subject to temptation. Jesus was subject to temptation, too.

So there is a presumption that every person sins.

This is a fact, a reality. This goes with being human. We come into the world with the effects of original sin. The mind is darkened. The will is weakened. If there were no sins, there would be no reason for the heavenly Father to send his Son, Jesus, to redeem us. But that is precisely why Christ came, to pay the price of our sins, to restore a loving relationship with the heavenly Father.

What constitutes a sin? How do people know they have committed sins?

God designs, devises and defines the relationship we are to have with him. He expresses his holy will. The absolute, ultimate norm of morality is the will of God. The good Lord did not create the world, step back and have nothing to do with it. God has communicated with all human beings from the beginning of time.

What makes something good? What makes something evil?

Whatever conforms to the will of God is good. Whatever does not conform to the will of God is bad.

It's that simple?

Yes! In general, God's will is expressed in his commandments. Jesus articulated God's holy will in his life and in his teachings. If we know Jesus Christ, we know the will of the heavenly Father. Jesus continues to guide all of us through his Church. So we are blessed in knowing the will of God. Embracing God's will, endorsing God's will in our lives, is challenging.

How are we tempted? What is a temptation?

Temptation is an attraction to sin. In one way or another we are challenged to choose some manner of conduct other than God's holy will. This has been going on since the Garden of Eden. The devil whispers there is happiness in sin. He convinced Eve that if she defied God, and ate the forbidden fruit, she would be like God. Eve knew better. However, she allowed herself to be persuaded, knowingly and willingly. The same can be said for Adam. The same can be said for all of us. We are responsible for our decisions. People may offer the excuse that "The devil made me do it", but that's a cop-out.

The devil is real, not just a Halloween character?

Definitely! Jesus cast out devils from people who were possessed. The devil is a fallen angel. There was a trial. Angels were tempted. Some defied God. They were condemned to hell, driven out of heaven by St. Michael, the archangel. The devil is called Satan, or Lucifer. The gospel sometimes refers to many devils, legions of devils.

Does the devil have power to compel someone to commit sin?

No! With the grace of God, all temptations can be overcome. With sin, there has to be consent freely given.

But is the devil the source of all temptation? Does God allow the devil to act freely?

St. Matthew's gospel tells of Christ's temptation. This took place in a wilderness area. Jesus prayed and fasted for 40 days and nights. Christ was hungry and the devil tried to persuade him to turn stones into bread. Jesus countered by saying, "One does not live by bread alone, / but by every word that comes forth from the mouth of God." Then, the devil enticed Christ throw himself down from the temple's height, but Christ countered "You shall not put the Lord, your God, to the test." The devil showed Christ the kingdoms of this world in all their magnificence. Satan offered this treasure if Christ would worship him. "The Lord, your God, you shall worship / and him alone shall you serve." (Matthew 4:1-11) Finally the devil left him.

They say the sources of temptation are: the world, the flesh and the devil. In other words, temptations arise from the desire of the eyes, the desire of the flesh and the pride of life.

So a would-be convert to Christianity has to develop self-control. This is part of the training, part of the process of conversion.

Temptations are not going to go away. A sincere follower of Christ is expected to overcome temptation, to avoid occasions that would easily lead into sin. When a person asks for baptism, it does not mean he or she is already perfect. But it does mean that there is a reasonable expectation that Christ can be followed. The lifestyle of the convert must be in harmony with Jesus Christ.

Give me an example of an occasion of sin.

Well, it certainly is not a good idea for an alcoholic to hang around a saloon. If teenagers run with those who use narcotics, heroin or cocaine, they had better find new friends and companions. Single men and women who keep company may endanger their souls by throwing moral restraint and caution to the wind. Many times circumstances are more conducive in disobeying of God's holy will.

Chapter Sixteen

GOD'S PLAN

You seem to be quite convinced in what you say. How can you be so sure? Is there but one way to go to God?

Centuries ago the psalmist writing under the inspiration of the Holy Spirit says that he has love for God's law, but detests those who are half-hearted, or divided in their hearts. (Psalm 119:113) In our relationship with God, it is good to be confident. Either God has communicated or he has not. If God has communicated, there is no room for error on the part of God. And God wants us to have confidence in him. He encourages us to trust in him.

Those with faith seem to have something intangible. They appear to know where they are going in life.

People who know God are blessed. The are not like "sheep without a Shepherd", as Jesus expresses it. And Jesus once said, "Whoever has seen me has seen the Father." John 14:9 He was talking to Philip, one of his apostles. If anyone is seeking God, he will find God in Jesus Christ. There is no Plan B. Christ said, "I am the way, and the truth and the life. No one comes to the Father except through me." (John 14:6)

Shall I read about Christ in the bible? Take out books from the library? What is the recommended procedure?

Jesus Christ is still with us. He is present in the Church and operates through his Church. Every Catholic parish welcomes those who are

interested in Jesus Christ and his Church. From the beginning of the Church, there have been instructions and opportunities to learn. In the early centuries they called it the catechumenate. Those seeking to learn were called catechumens. Men and women joined with Christians who prayed and worshipped with them. There was a gradual orientation or indoctrination. The course might have taken a year or two, depending on the person. Today, parish priests and qualified parishioners give instructions. There is a program called, the Rite of Christian Initiation for Adults, the RCIA.

I suppose there is an advantage in a well-planned program to find answers and to become acquainted with the faith community.

God is certainly mindful of the sincere of heart seeking him. There are souls who attempt to pursue God on their own. But this solo effort can be very challenging and confusing. This was illustrated a number of years ago in a book entitled, "Seven Storey Mountain" by Thomas Merton. He was a man who went from religion to religion. He eventually became a Catholic, and in time, a priest and a Trappist monk.

There are many voices in the world. But the voices are discordant, a veritable babble. Perhaps you know the biblical story of the Tower of Babel. Folks tried to build a tower to heaven and ended up speaking different languages. Today there is a plethora of religions. There are many Christian sects and denominations. Jesus Christ and his teachings are not preached in a uniform, consistent manner. The fullness of Christ is found in the Catholic Church. As Vatican Council II states, "For it is through Christ's Catholic Church alone, which is the universal help toward salvation, that the fullness of the means of salvation can be obtained." (3#)

Will the real Jesus Christ please stand up?
Authenticity is paramount when eternity hangs in the balance.

So you recommend participation in a local parish program, an RCIA?
This is a first step. You will find personal interest. Hopefully the good example of the parishioners will be inspirational. They will be praying for you, too.

Do all Catholic parishes teach in the same way?
Basically, yes! Catholics throughout the world profess the same creed.

Will I find the real Christ?
Faith is a gift from God. It is a grace that God wants to give. Information and inspiration are in tandem. The mind and will are fused. It is important to note that Christ and his Church are one. Jesus acts in his Church. Finding Christ is also to find his Church. Faith is expressed in time and in place. Faith is embraced and expressed in the Christian community.

Tell me about parishes? These are individual faith communities. Some seem to be more active than others. My friends say they often prefer to attend one particular church because the music and song is livelier, or the preaching is more pertinent, or the parishioners friendlier. They like the priests in one parish more than in another.
Their observations are typical, and no doubt, accurate. But all parishes embrace Jesus Christ. Some parishes are small. City parishes may have parishioners by the thousands. Some have Catholic schools. Other parishes do not have schools. But to be truly grounded a person's faith must be centered in Jesus Christ himself. If you are seeking God, realize that your mind and heart must be centered in Christ himself. Then, when challenges and adversities come your way, you will be sustained in your relationship with the heavenly Father.

In Christ our relationship with the heavenly Father is well founded, solid, like a rock.
Jesus said, "Everyone who listens to these words of mine and acts on them will be like a wise man who built his house on rock. The rain fell, the floods came, and the winds blew and buffeted his house. But it did not collapse...". (Matthew 7:24-25) Christ went on to say that those who do not act on his words will be like fools who built their house on sand. Eventually the hostile elements cause it to collapse.

You surely are emphatic about a person's belief in Christ.
No one will ever be mislead following Jesus Christ. And Christ can not be followed without following his Church. Individuals in the Church

may be misleading. In the course of history there have been those who have spoken or acted in the name of religion. Some have not embodied the true teachings of Jesus Christ in their missions. This is merely a caution. It is imperative to be able to distinguish between Jesus Christ and his Church from those who have proven themselves to be otherwise.

Why are you so careful about distinguishing the Church from the people in the Church?

Those with chips on their shoulders are quite ready to leave the Church and consequently, to ready to leave Christ. Jesus selected twelve apostles from his many disciples. Eleven persevered. Judas betrayed Christ. When some men and women become angry, or feel they have been wronged, they walk away. No one should throw the baby out with the bath water.

Well, suppose a parishioner has a fight with the pastor of a parish. He or she might feel very uncomfortable attending Mass on Sunday.

Disagreements are not new. They go all the way back through the centuries. The Acts of the Apostles tells how St. Paul confronted opposition in more than one place. One of the Works of Mercy is to bear wrongs patiently. There is no better example than the patience of Jesus Christ. Although Christ was innocent, he was crucified for all our sins. Parishioners, uncomfortable worshipping in one parish, might frequent another. "Blessed are the peacemakers…".

Were not the apostles martyrs for Christ? The threat of death did not deter them from remaining loyal.

Tradition says that Peter was crucified upside down. Paul was beheaded. James was thrown from the Temple's height. All won the crown of martyrdom, except John. He died a natural death. Christians have to take up their own crosses in imitation of Christ. "Blessed are you when they insult you and persecute you and utter every kind of evil against you [falsely] because of me. Rejoice and be glad for your reward will be great in heaven." Matthew 5:11-12) God's plan of salvation has a great price.

Chapter Seventeen

BITS AND PIECES

It is quite clear that if someone wishes to know God's plan for salvation, he really has to know Jesus Christ. From what you say, learning about Christ and following his teachings present serious challenges. The ordinary person knows some details of Jesus' life, but does not have a comprehensive picture. Most of us know bits and pieces.

Some details of Christ's birth are familiar. While Christmas is increasingly secular in its celebration, the traditional carols tell the story. "O Town of Bethlehem", "Away In A Manger", "Silent Night" and "We Three Kings" are songs aired on radio and sung by choirs. The infant Jesus was born of the Virgin Mary, in Bethlehem, which is 6 miles from Jerusalem. The town was crowded with people coming to register for the Roman census ordered by Emperor Caesar Augustus. So there was no room in the inn. Shepherds guarding the flocks in near-by fields were notified by angels singing, "Glory to God in the highest..." The shepherds came to the cave and paid Christ homage.

I thought it was a stable.

It was a small cave used to house animals. The site is located beneath the Church of the Nativity in Bethlehem. Tourists and pilgrims are surprised to see how small it is.

And the Wise Men or Magi came to worship, too.

Yes, but in all probability, Mary, Joseph and the Christ-child, had found other lodgings when they arrived. The Magi were astrologers. They are also called kings. They followed a star, journeying from the east. They stopped in Jerusalem to learn more precisely where the newborn king was born. King Herod perceived Christ's birth as a threat to his kingship. When the Magi did not return to inform Herod of their visit to Bethlehem, he panicked. He ordered the death of all newborn male infants in the Bethlehem area. It is estimated that about 30 babies were slaughtered by Herod's soldiers. This feast of the Holy Innocents is celebrated on December 28th. The Magi may have arrived as late as two years after Christ's birth.

Are all these details in the bible?
Many of the details are related in the gospels of Matthew, and Luke. Scripture scholars refer to this history of Christ's early life as the infancy narrative. Tradition plays a part, too. For example, the gospels do not say that there were 3 Wise Men. The number three seems to correspond to the three gifts that they brought: frankincense, gold and myrrh. Their names, Casper, Melchior and Balthasar, are not in the bible, but probably were ascribed to them in the middle ages.

Will reading the bible assist us in coordinating our knowledge of Jesus?
The Church encourages reading the bible prayerfully. Many editions of the bible have footnotes and commentaries. The instructions or classes provided in parish programs help to organize our thoughts. The bible is not a book, but a collection of 73 books. The Old Testament consists in the 46 books written before the time of Christ. The New Testament consists in the 27 books written after Christ. The books were written to assist people in their journey of faith and in knowing their relationship with God. All the books were written under the inspiration of God. But they were written at different times, in different places, for different purposes, by different human authors. The word of God needs interpretation and that's why Jesus instituted the Church.

So it is possible for bible readers to draw inexact conclusions about God and about Jesus Christ.

Yes! This happens all the time. And again, that's why Jesus instituted his Church. History bears this out. There were heresies from the earliest times. The Councils of Nicaea, 325 AD, Constantinople, 381 AD, Ephesus, 431, AD, and Chalcedon, 451 AD addressed errors relating to the Trinity, Christ's divinity and Christ's humanity.

So what do you advise?
Select a Catholic bible, one that has an Imprimatur within its first few pages. This indicates that the bible's version corresponds to the earliest manuscripts. All the books have the authorization of the Church. In the early centuries there were other writings that claimed to be authentically God's word, or were so presumed. While they may have merit, they are not officially on the Church's canon. Catholic bibles differ from Protestant bibles in the number of books and in their translation. Originally the books in the bible were written in Hebrew , that is the Old Testament books, and in Greek, that is the New Testament books, with the exception of Matthew's gospel (Hebrew).

Shall I start at the beginning of the bible, the Book of Genesis?
It will probably be better to begin with St. Matthew's gospel. Do not hurry through the gospel. Ask questions. See how your knowledge of Jesus corresponds.

Then, shall I continue with St. Mark's gospel?
Yes! Some details vary from St. Matthew's gospel and the other gospels. But the details do not contradict one another. Eventually read St. Luke's gospel and St. John's gospel. The gospels of Matthew, Mark and Luke are called synoptic gospels. They are similar in many ways.

What about St. John's gospel?
The apostle, John, special friend of Jesus, wrote his gospel, three letters or epistles, and the Book of Revelation. His gospel differs from the synoptic gospels. It is described as highly literary and symbolic. The other gospels were already in use before John's. John's was completed between 90 and 100 AD. In his prologue John "proclaims Jesus as the preexistent and incarnate Word of God who has revealed the Father to us." (NAB commentary) John cites certain "signs" or miracles of Christ. His

purpose is clear. "But these are written so that you may [come to] believe that Jesus is the Messiah, the Son of God, and through this belief you may have life in his name." (John 20:30) John is explicit in his emphasis that Christ is divine.

Are the gospels considered biographical?

They surely present the life and teachings of Jesus. They are considered historical in a sense, although not history in the usual sense. The apostles, in communicating about Christ, preached and taught before they wrote. Their intent was to present Christ so that both the Jews and the non-Jews, the gentiles, would come to believe. At a point of time, God, the Father, intervened in our world by sending his Son, the second Person of the Trinity. It was their intention to show by words and by writings that Jesus is the Messiah, the Savior, the Redeemer.

And those who came to believe began to follow Christ. They became Christians?

The Acts of the Apostles tells about Barnabas and Paul communicating the "good news" in Antioch. "For a whole year they met with the church and taught a large number of people, and it was in Antioch that the disciples were first called Christians." (Acts 11:26)

What shall I look for when I read the New Testament?

Ask God to enlighten you. Pray for wisdom and understanding. Read the gospels prayerfully rather than academically. Those who seek God need grace to assist them, to dispose their minds and hearts. Jesus is "the way, the truth and the life". You will be seeking Jesus, and no one comes to the Father except through Jesus.

So I will be seeking the "good news". Will I be evangelized?

Hopefully, yes! The word, evangelization, comes from the Latin word for gospel. And the gospel proclaims Jesus Christ. "This proclamation reaches it full development when it is listened to, accepted and assimilated, and when it evokes a genuine commitment in the one who has received it. Those whose lives have been transformed enter a community which is itself a sign of transformation, a sign of newness of life: it is the

Church, the visible sacrament of salvation." (Paulist Summary #23 Evangelii Nuntiandi)

Chapter Eighteen

ACTS, HABITS AND CHARACTER

Presumably those who are evangelized undergo a transformation. Does this happen during the parish instruction program?

Spiritual transformation is virtually imperceptible. It is like the growth of trees. Day after day there is change. A man or woman seeking God probably experiences a longing for fulfillment, a desire for the good, the beautiful and the true. In effect they long for God. The grace of God is working within their souls even before they enroll in an instruction program. Hopefully their personal advancement is brought along as they learn and practice the faith.

Describe what might happen in an RCIA parish program.

Catechumens, those under instruction, meet others who are pursuing God. During classes they might share experiences. They have the benefit of the questions raised by others. Usually those taking the courses are accompanied by sponsors, relatives, acquaintances or parishioners. Sponsors must be practicing Catholics, living the Christian life, attending Mass faithfully and receiving the sacraments. It's helpful to have a friend to rely on. Catechumens are more comfortable with this arrangement. Sponsors are encouraged to pray for them.

Conversion takes time. Transformation does not happen over night. Do we leave our wicked past behind us and cross over the bridge?

Yes! And I can see that you remember the lyrics of the song about crossing over the bridge. **With God's grace men and women are born again, baptized in the Lord. During the transition period, good habits are formed.**

For example?
Many people are not in the habit of worshipping. They have not been observing the first and third commandments about adoring God and keeping the Lord's Day holy.

Is this obligation for every Sunday?
Yes! And this also includes participating in Mass on Holy Days of Obligation that occur on weekdays.

During the weeks and months we are in training.
Repeated good acts form good habits. These are called virtues. Good habits facilitate our lives. Those who want to excel in music, in sports…in almost anything, have to practice, practice, and practice. The same is true as we attempt to cooperate with the grace of God and strive for perfection.

Some people may have many good habits. Others may not be living good lives and have several bad habits. I gather that conversion is not the same for everyone. Do men and women sometime think that it is not possible for them to change?
There is hope for everyone. God's grace is sufficient. It took years for St. Augustine to experience conversion. Mary Magdalene turned her life around when she met Jesus. In a sense, sinners misplace their love. Then, they discover God. They begin to love God for God's sake. Of course, conversion and perfection are not instantaneous. It often takes prayer and penance. Sincere people struggle with themselves, going against the grain.

Those who come from loving homes and families must have an advantage. Parents who correct and discipline their sons and daughters bless them tremendously. Still, I'll bet there are countless numbers of families where religion is hardly mentioned.

Mothers and fathers who share their belief in God provide a foundation in the minds and hearts of their children. There is something to build on. Morality is defined. Good and evil are articulated.

Unwittingly parents set an example. They provide models for life.

There is an axiom that epitomizes the process of development. "Sow and act, and you reap a habit. Sow a habit, and you reap a character. Sow a character, and you reap a destiny." (source unknown)

All of us are free and we are invited to make right choices. It is wisdom to make choices in harmony with God's will.

What are some of the other habits a person might work on if they were pursuing God? If a man or woman were participating in a parish instruction program, what would be expected of them?

Daily prayer! This is a wonderful habit. Indispensable! We talk to God. The way we talk to God is usually to ask, to praise, to thank and to express sorrow for our sins. We are in a relationship with God. In the morning, we pray for God's graces and blessings for the day. We offer our day to God. May everything we do give God glory. In the evening we thank God for all the good things that happen to us. We may make an act of contrition, begging pardon for our sins.

Catholics memorize prayers, don't they?

Yes, they do and this is a good idea. It is recommended that adults in an RCIA program commit to memory the Our Father, the Hail Mary, and the Glory Be prayer. These, along with the Act of Contrition, are standard. We should add the Apostles Creed, too. It is expected that children who prepare for their first Holy Communion come to know these prayers by heart. These are not difficult to memorize. When they are recited out loud on a daily basis, the prayers become part of one's routine.

But we are free to pray spontaneously, too. Right?

Certainly! This is encouraged. But do not minimize the importance of memorizing the traditional prayers. Be mindful that the Our Father, the Lord's Prayer, was given to us by Jesus himself. The Hail Mary flows from scripture, the Angel Gabriel greeting Christ's blessed mother.

Memorized prayers facilitate our participation other devotions. The Rosary, for example.

What about meditation?

An excellent practice! There are different methods of this mental prayer. One commonly used is to imagine you are with Christ in a particular place or situation. What would it be like if you were a visitor at the stable in Bethlehem when Jesus was born? What would be your feelings standing beneath Christ's cross? There are meditation books that might illustrate. Some folks might like to be silent and say with Samuel in the bible, "Speak, LORD, for your servant is listening." (1 Samuel 3:9) Don't expect to hear voices. God ordinarily does not communicate that way. But it is always good to ask God to enlighten you and to give you the strength to fulfill his holy will.

I suppose there are other bad habits that do not belong in our relationship with God. Among them I'm thinking of vulgar language, taking God's name in vain, poor mouthing other people and so on.

We are more conscious of our faults the closer we come to God. It is the grace of God working within us. We want to be better persons for God's sake. In a way, it is like children wanting their parents to be happy with them. And we are all God's children.

Jesus must spell out how we should act, how we should relate to one another.

Christ is our teacher. He loves us beyond our imagination. When we grow in love for Christ, we want to do things his way. There is a step-up in our relationship when we try to be good and to avoid evil, not because we dread the loss of heaven and the pains of hell. We want to embrace God's will simply because we love him. The transformation has begun within us.

The picture is becoming quite clear. We really need to know Jesus Christ.

He wants to be part of our lives. We wish to identify with Christ. There is great joy and great peace in our hearts.

Chapter Nineteen

A True Picture of Christ

Tell me about Jesus Christ. We really do not know what he looked like. Artists paint him in long robes with a beard and flowing hair. Christ is portrayed in films, but these are recreations, subject to the screen writers and directors.

No one knows Christ's physical characteristics. These are not described in the gospels. The gospels were about who Jesus was and what he accomplished. But we have favorite paintings of Christ. Christians proclaim their faith in Christ by hanging the pictures in their homes. Objects of devotion are helpful. Reading the four gospels prayerfully helps us to form pictures in our minds. Matthew, Mark, Luke and John tell us about Christ's life, where he lived and where he traveled. They describe his many miracles. He encountered opposition from the religious establishment of his day, the scribes, the chief priests and the Pharisees. How he reacted and related to those in his life tells us about Christ himself.

We do not know much about his childhood, do we?

The gospels tell us about Christ's birth and his journey to Jerusalem with Mary and Joseph when he was about twelve years old. Remember that the apostles and evangelists brought the "good news" orally. They were like Christ, the teacher, who spoke and addressed people personally. Jesus did not write his lessons. Only after 30 or more years did the human authors of the gospels record the teachings and events in Christ's life with

pen and ink. The essence of their communication was that Jesus was God and man, the Messiah.

But he lived his entire life in Israel. There wasn't much travelling.

That's true. There is an incident where Jesus was in pagan territory, near Tyre and Sidon. Travel was by foot or beast of burden. The gospels focus on Christ's last three years of life here on earth. The evangelists relate what happened during Christ's public ministry. Israel is still where it has been for centuries, at the eastern end of the Mediterranean Sea. It is about the size of Massachusetts and Connecticut together, 150 miles long and 40 miles wide. There are beaches and mountains and valleys and fertile plains. The Sea of Galilee is in the north. The Jordan River twists its way from the Sea of Galilee to the south and meets the Dead Sea. Many bibles feature maps of the area. It is helpful to find the places mentioned in the bible: Nazareth, where Jesus grew up; Bethany where he visited his friends; Jerusalem where he was crucified and rose from the dead.

It would be wonderful to visit the Holy Land and trace the footsteps of Christ.

Religious pilgrimages are available. Tourists and pilgrims read the gospel passages at the sites where Christ walked on the water and where he gave sight to the blind.

This helps to make their faith more real. It is experiential. They connect sites and locations to the gospel selections proclaimed at Mass on Sunday. They may read about Capernum while sitting among the ruins of that town. They may look across the Sea of Galilee and imagine the apostles fishing. All the while those on pilgrimage pray that they may understand and appreciate. They are confirmed in their faith.

They walk literally in the footsteps of Christ.

Not everyone has the privilege and opportunity to journey to the Holy Land. Everyone is encouraged to follow Christ. He invites us. "Come follow me." There is an invitation to become one of his disciples.

We do form opinions of people by what they say and what they do. Unwittingly we relate to them as we judge their character. I imagine we learn much about Christ by studying his teachings.

Jesus, like all good teachers and preachers, used examples and comparisons. God, who has communicated from the beginning of time, knows how to speak in terms that are understandable. The New Testament does not contain every word that Jesus spoke. And as St. John reminds us, all Christ's miracles are not recorded in his gospel. But the New Testament provides us with some 39 parables, short stories that lead us to moral conclusions. These reflect Jesus Christ himself.

What are some of the parables?

We mentioned one a little earlier. The one about the wise man building his house on rock and the foolish man building his house on sand.

Jesus also told a story about being prepared to meet God. There were five wise bridesmaids and five foolish bridesmaids. The wise ones took sufficient oil for their lamps. The foolish ones did not. In those days, it was not uncommon for grooms to delay and be late. There were no wrist watches then.

I remember the parable about the prodigal son. This must be a favorite among people. It has to do with God's forgiveness. We all need to be forgiven.

St. Matthew records this story. One son squandered his inheritance in riotous living. He came to his senses during a famine and while he was feeding pigs. Repentant, the prodigal son returns home. His father sees him from afar and runs out to welcome him. Jesus is saying that there is great joy in the conversion of a sinner. (Matthew 21: 28-32)

Is there any kind of description of Christ in the New Testament?

St. Paul writes to the Christians in Colossae, a town about 100 miles east of Ephesus, which is in the territory of modern Turkey. Speaking of Jesus, Paul says, "He is the image of the invisible God, / the firstborn of all creation. / For in him were created all things in heaven and on earth, / the visible and the invisible, / whether thrones or dominions or principalities or powers; all things all things were created through him

and for him. / He is before all things, / and in him all things hold together. / He is the head of the body, the church. / He is the beginning, the firstborn of the dead, / that in all things he himself might be preeminent. / For in him all the fullness was pleased to dwell, / and through him to reconcile all things for him, / making peace through the blood of his cross / [through him], whether those on earth or those in heaven." (Colossians 1:15-20)

This is a profound description. This is the kind of description that deserves examination and meditation. Paul declares that Jesus is divine.

Yes! Paul makes that clear. Nevertheless, those who wish to know Christ well, more intimately, need to spend time reading the New Testament. If we can keep in mind that Jesus is God, it will dispose us to observe that everything he says and does is perfect. God does not make mistakes. God can not deceive, nor be deceived.

I am beginning to feel that coming to know Christ is an overwhelming experience.

Our appreciation grows. It develops. And if our minds and hearts are properly disposed, we may realize the depth of God's love for us.

This is not something that many of us realize. We take life for granted. Our knowledge of what has happened in the centuries past is so limited, and often, so uncoordinated. We hear it said that we are to love God, but it is easier to love family members and people around us. God is considered to be distant. Evidently we do not relate well. We do not attribute to God all that we are and all that we have.

Jesus is one of us. He is human, as well as divine. He relates perfectly with us. We can relate to him. The coming of this Divine Person consists of love beyond description. Coming to know Jesus is a blessed enlightenment. He is our reason for living. Our raison d'etre. Christ mediates for us. He is the one and only Mediator between heaven and earth, between ourselves and his heavenly Father.

This promises to be a great awakening.

"The people who walked in darkness / have seen a great light!" (Isaiah 9:1)

"Open up your hearts and let the sun shine in". Lyrics of a song! **Jesus is the "Light of the World".**

Chapter Twenty

THAT YOU MAY COME TO BELIEVE

Jesus walked about the dusty roads of Israel, talking and associating with people. They saw the signs or experienced the miracles that he performed. According to St. John's gospel that you quote, there were many other miracles simply not cited in this scripture.

There are 37 miracles described in the 4 gospels, Matthew, Mark, Luke and John. Some of the identical miracles are recorded in the different gospels. The apostle, John says, "These are written so that you may [come to] believe that Jesus is the Messiah, the Son of God..." (John 20:30)

So Christ was a miracle worker.

Yes! He demonstrated his divine power. In other words, he showed by his own power that he was God. After Christ's resurrection some miracles happened when the apostles invoked Christ's name. There is an incident recorded in the Acts of the Apostles. Peter and John encountered a man crippled from birth. He was begging alms at Jerusalem's Beautiful Gate. "Peter said, 'I have neither silver nor gold, but what I do have I give you: in the name of Jesus Christ the Nazorean, [rise and] walk." (Acts 3:6) He took the man by the hand and the man walked. He was cured.

Why were the apostles able to effect miracles?

Because God wanted them to be instruments of his grace. It was as if God was giving approval to their preaching and their communicating of the gospel. The Church was in its early stages of growth. These dedicated men went from country to country. Those listening to them and witnessing the miracles came to believe. But note well. They did not have power on their own. Miracles happened in the name of Jesus.

On the other hand, you are saying that when Jesus gave an order that was humanly impossible to fulfill, it happened.

Exactly! St. Mark speaks of a leper who called upon Christ for a cure of his incurable disease. " 'If you wish, you can make me clean.' Moved with pity, he stretched out his hand, touched him, and said, 'I do will it. Be made clean.' The leprosy left him immediately, and he was made clean." (Mark 1:40-42)

That fellow must have been very happy.

Jesus cured many people. His fame spread throughout the land. Crowds followed him. They carried their sick and laid them at Jesus' feet. There were times when the numbers pursuing Christ were overwhelming. His compassion moved him to extend his blessings to those suffering from a variety of afflictions.

What are some of the other miracles of Jesus?

The lame walked, the blind saw, and the deaf heard. Jesus walked on the water. He calmed the stormy sea. On one occasion Christ multiplied five barley loaves and two fish. More than five thousand people were fed and there were twelve baskets of fragments left over.

This is impressive. And you say that he performed these miracles on his own power.

Yes! Unmistakably with his own power as God. The healing of a paralytic illustrates this clearly. A great crowd gathered at Christ's dwelling in Capernum. Friends of a paralyzed man tried to reach Christ but were unable. Determined to bring the paralytic to Jesus, they opened the roof and lowered him on a mat at Jesus' feet. Christ said to him, " 'Child, your sins are forgiven.' Now some of the scribes were sitting there asking themselves, 'Why does this man speak that way? He is

blaspheming. Who but God alone can forgive sins?' Jesus immediately knew in his mind what they were thinking to themselves, so he said, 'Why are you thinking such things in your hearts? Which is easier to say to the paralytic, 'Your sins are forgiven', or to say, 'Rise, pick up your mat and walk?' But that you may know that the Son of Man has authority to forgive sins on earth '---he said to the paralytic, 'I say to you, rise, pick up your mat, and go home.' He rose, picked up his mat at once, and went away in the sight of everyone." (Mark 2:5-12)

Some people then, may have said, "This is too good to be true."

That is a possibility. Some folks are reluctant to accept that which is proven. The evidence leads them to a conclusion, but they remain skeptical. It is helpful to remember that Christ's miracles were performed in broad daylight. There were no smoke and mirrors. The thousands of men and women on the mountainside when Jesus multiplied the loaves and fishes had food to eat. Their stomachs were filled. There were no fast-food restaurants nor catering services available. The many men and women who experienced cures also testified to the miracles. These were people known to others; friends, relatives, neighbors. They were aware of their conditions for years.

Did Christ claim to be God?

Definitely! That's why he was accused of blasphemy. This was one of the charges made against him when he was brought before the Jewish court, the Sanhedrin.

Claiming to be God is extraordinary. Fort someone to say this is almost unbelievable.

The coming of God to our world is unique and wonderful. This is the most important event in history. But Jesus claimed to be God, and he proved it.

Did Jesus have power over life and death?

There are three miracles where Jesus called people back to life. On one occasion when Christ and his apostles entered a town called Nain, they encountered a funeral procession. The only son of a widow was being carried to his grave. Jesus was moved with pity. He stopped the bearers

and said, "'Young man, I tell you, arise.' The dead man sat up and began to speak, and Jesus gave him to his mother." (Luke 7:14-15) And Matthew, Mark and Luke all tell about Christ restoring the life of a 12 year old girl. She was the daughter of a synagogue official named Jairus. He sought out Jesus, tell him that his little girl was gravely ill. When they arrived at Jairus' home the crowd gathered there told them that she had already died. Jesus said she was not dead, but only sleeping. They ridiculed him. Christ took Peter, James and John along with the girl's parents into her room. He grasped the daughter by the hand and said, " 'Child, arise!' Her breath returned and she immediately arose. He then directed that she be given something to eat. Her parents were astounded..." (Luke 8:54-56)

What is the third incident where Jesus calls someone back to life?
This is the celebrated miracle of Lazarus. This gospel selection from St. John is probably proclaimed at funeral Masses more than any other. Martha, Mary and their brother, Lazarus, lived in Bethany, about 2 miles from Jerusalem. They were friends of Christ and he visited their home. Lazarus died. Christ was some distance away. Word reached him, but he did not arrive in Bethany until 2 days later. Martha met him and said, "Lord, if you had been here, my brother would not have died." Jesus assured her. "Your brother will rise." Martha said to him, "I know he will rise, in the resurrection on the last day." Jesus told her, "I am the resurrection and the life; whoever believes in me, even if he dies, will live, and everyone who lives and believes in me will never died." (John 11: 21-27)
Christ asked to be taken to Lazarus tomb. There was a stone across the entrance. As he stood before the tomb together with the crowd of mourners, Jesus said, "Take away the stone." Martha reminded him that her brother was already dead for four days and there would be a stench. Jesus prayed to his heavenly Father, and then, commanded, "Lazarus, come out!" And the dead man came out, still wrapped in his burial cloths.

That was certainly dramatic. It is easy to see why many people came to believe in Christ.
God provides a basis for our belief. There is a foundation to our faith. It rests on facts. These were real events. They are not fairy stories or

myths. And notice Christ's words to Martha. "I am the resurrection and the life..." The greatest miracle is his own resurrection.

Chapter Twenty-One

A SENSE OF AWE

It is understandable that Christ's fame spread throughout the land. His miracles are many and varied. People must have had a feeling of awe of what was happening.

St. Matthew in his gospel tells us that once Jesus and his apostles were out on the Sea of Galilee when a fierce storm arose. Christ commanded the tempest and calmed the raging waters. "The men were amazed and said 'What sort of a man is this whom even the winds and the sea obey?'" (Matthew 8:27)

St. Mark records an incident in the synagogue in Capernum. A man was possessed by an unclean spirit. Jesus said "Quiet! Come out of him!" The unclean spirit convulsed him and with a loud cry came out of him. All were amazed and asked one another and asked, "What is this? A new teaching with authority. He commands even the unclean spirits and they obey him." (Mark 1:21-28)

One can only imagine how deeply people were impressed. I'll bet a chill ran down their spines.

When Jesus brought the widow's son back to life in Nain, the young fellow began to speak. St. Luke says, "Fear seized them all, and they glorified God, exclaiming, 'A great prophet has arisen in our midst,' and 'God has visited his people' ". (Luke 7:16)

There was another incident when a man with an unclean spirit could not be subdued even with chains and shackles. Apparently there were legions of demons. Christ commanded the devils to come out of the man and enter a herd of swine. Then, the herd of swine rushed down a steep embankment and plunged into the lake. When the people from a nearby town and surrounding area came out to see what happened, they saw the formerly possessed man sitting quietly at Jesus's feet. They learned about the fate of the herd of swine. "The entire population of the region of the Gerasenes asked Jesus to leave them because they were seized with great fear." (Luke 8:37)

Those, who encountered Jesus witnessed his super-human powers. They could not help but be impressed. Awesome is an adjective insufficient to describe the happenings.

When Jesus restored the daughter of Jairus to life, St. Mark tells us, "The girl, a child of 12 arose immediately and walked around. [At that] they were utterly astounded." (Mark 5:42)

There is no doubt that folks were amazed, astounded and filled with fear. The miracles of Jesus stirred their very souls. In varying degrees they experienced the presence of God. The psalmist tells us that the fear of the Lord is the beginning of wisdom. Profound respect wells up in those who are of sincere of heart.

What were you hinting at when you said people experienced the presence of God in varying degrees? Were there folks who failed to see the divine dimension in Christ's miracles?

Once Jesus cured a demoniac who was blind and mute. The Pharisees, who were part of the religious opposition, belittled the miracle saying, "This man drives out demons only by the power of Beelzebul, the prince of demons." (Matthew 12:24) And the scribes, those versed in the Mosaic Law, also accused Christ of being in league with the devil. "The scribes who had come from Jerusalem said, 'He is possessed by Beelzebul,' and 'By the prince of demons he drives out demons.' " (Mark 3:22)

So even miracles failed to convince everyone. If Jesus is truly God, to be accused of cooperating with the devil, was blatantly outrageous. Is that what they mean by "hardened hearts"?

God never compels anyone to act any way but freely. But he also provides the grace we need to understand. Dispositions of mind and heart are of the utmost importance. Once Christ's disciples approached him and asked, "Who is the greatest in the kingdom of heaven?" He called a child over, placed it in their midst, and said, "Amen, I say to you, unless you turn and become like children, you will not enter the kingdom of heaven. Whoever humbles himself like this child is the greatest in the kingdom of heaven. And whoever receives one child such as this in my name receives me." (Matthew 18:1-5)

You are saying that we must be childlike in our belief. Doesn't this lend itself to gullibility and naivete?
We must be childlike, not childish. Consider how a child trusts his father or his mother. He walks hand in hand. Children are beautiful in their innocence. They do not a hidden agenda or ulterior motives.
Those who are seeking God will find God through Jesus Christ. Jesus gave glory to the Father. "I give praise to you, Father, Lord of heaven and earth, for although you have hidden these things from the wise and the learned you have revealed them to the childlike. Yes, Father, such has been your gracious will. All things have been handed over to me by my Father. No one knows the Son except the Father, and no one knows the Father except the Son and anyone to whom the Son wishes to reveal him." (Matthew 11:25-27)

I take it that anyone who approaches the heavenly Father with anything but humility is not of the right frame of mind.
Humility and truth are virtually identical. Jesus says, "I am the way, and the truth and the life…". (John 14:6) He, also says, "…learn from me, for I am meek and humble of heart." (Matthew 11:29)

Christ performed miracles to prove that he was God and to provide a basis for belief. At the same time, it is inevitable that the people's reaction would be a sense of awe. I would think this lends itself to a worship of Christ, a worship of God.
In the Christmas carol, O Come All You Faithful, the lyrics follow with "O Come, let us adore him". Christians sing familiar and traditional songs at Christmas time. These reflect their belief. They worship in music

and song. At the feast of the Epiphany, the Magi brought gifts of gold, frankincense and myrrh. They rendered homage to the newborn Christ-child. Awe and worship do go hand in hand. We bow down before God. This is a proper posture, a proper disposition. God is our Father, our Creator. We are his children, his creatures.

Do people worship less today than they did in the past? There seems to be a rather casual approach to Sunday observance. Churches are often filled at Christmas and at Easter. On the other hand, there is to be plenty of room on other weekends.

Loosing sight of God is not anything new. The Old Testament tells of God calling his people back to him on many occasions. He raised up holy men and women who stirred their consciences. The psalms speak of those who molded idols from silver and gold, bowing down before them. We do become distracted. We devote ourselves to other gods, so to speak.

There is also a tendency on the part of some people to equate God with human beings. They may not intend to be offensive. They refer to God as "the man upstairs". They are very casual in their relationship with God, as if they had the right "to call the shots". It is always appropriate to have a deep respect for God, a profound reverence. As high as the heavens are above the earth, so superior is God to all of us.

As we progress in our journey of faith, a sense of awe befits us in our relationship with God. He does not want a paralyzing fear. St. John reminds us, "...everyone who loves, is begotten by God, and knows God. Whoever is without love, does not know God, for God is love." (1 John 4:7-8) "And whoever acknowledges that Jesus is the Son of God, God remains in him and he in God. We have come to know and to believe in the love God has for us." 1 John 4: 15-16) Our relationship with God should be a loving one, steeped in respect.

I am beginning to think that our love songs somehow flow from the bible. Romantic ballads are not always directed toward God, but the underlying theme of love seems unwittingly inherent. Lyrics like "What kind of fool am I who never fell in love?" and so on.

Jesus does not teach us to love the Lord with our whole heart and soul without good reason. With God's grace our entire being is coordinated, harmonized with God.

Chapter Twenty-Two

I AM THE RESURRECTION

Before Christ brought his friend, Lazarus, back to life, and when Martha spoke to him, Jesus answered her in an unexpected way. This surprised me. He said, "I am the resurrection and the life…". He portrayed himself in a peculiar and unique manner.
Only Christ could make that statement. He is "The Resurrection"!

I know you are going to explain that Christ rose from the dead. But the phraseology and his choice of expression differentiates his resurrection from the other miracles when he called others back to life. There appears to be a major distinction.
The emphasis is unmistakable. The event of Christ's resurrection is the cornerstone of the Christian faith. St. Paul points out that if Christ is not risen from the dead, then Paul's preaching is in vain. But, Paul declares that Jesus is truly risen. (Ref: 1 Corinthians 15:12-21) Christ's resurrection is the pinnacle of God's plan for everyone's eternal salvation. It is important to understand that Christ is not just another human being who was executed. He is a Divine Person, both God and man.

I am beginning to understand. Men and women have been tortured and put to death by cruel tyrants through the centuries. "Man's inhumanity to man" as they say. Christ's sufferings and death have an entirely different and greater dimension.

No one wants to minimize the barbarity and the hideousness of tortures inflicted on people during war while they were in prison and were held captive. There have been world leaders whose militant policies brought about wholesale destruction. Thousands, even millions, have suffered famine and starvation. Some may ask if they actually endured more than Christ who was crucified. In some cases they may have suffered horrendously. But Christ suffered more. His dignity is infinite. And his sufferings assumed the burden of all the sins of people in every age. He paid the price of everyone's sins from the beginning of time. His atonement is immeasurable. Jesus is a Divine Person.

Tell me now, is it true that as God, Christ did not suffer.

Correct! There is mystery here. Remember that God is not added to, nor diminished in any way at any time. God always was and always will be. That's what makes God, God. And in this sense, God is immutable. God does not change. God does not suffer. However, in this hypostatic union, this union of God and man, in the one Divine Person, Jesus suffered. If you were subject to pain and suffering, you would suffer as yourself, as a person. When Jesus was in the Garden of Olives and anticipating his ordeal he said, "My soul is sorrowful even to death." (Matthew 26:38) "He was in such agony and he prayed so fervently that his sweat became like drops of blood falling to the ground." (Luke 22:44)

So Christ actually knew what was coming. He anticipated his sufferings. His anxiety must have been unbearable.

When Christ and his disciples were at Caesaria Philippi, he predicted his passion. "He began to teach them that the Son of Man must suffer greatly and be rejected by the elders, the chief priests, and the scribes, and be killed, and rise after three days." (Mark 8:31) And again, when they were in Galilee, "He was teaching his disciples and telling them, 'The Son of Man is to be handed over to men and they will kill him, and three days after his death he will rise.' But they did not understand the saying, and they were afraid to question him." (Mark 9: 31-32)

Did they fail to understand what Jesus was saying because it was so unlikely?

In all probability they were so impressed and convinced of Christ's powers that they believed his was the Messiah. As the Messiah he was unstoppable. He calmed the stormy seas, he walked on the water, and he brought people back to life. St. Mark, who was a companion to St. Peter, probably heard Peter explain this as he preached. It is good to recall that the books in the New Testament were written several years after Christ's resurrection and ascension. Mark related Peter's words and sentiments. Scripture scholars believe that Mark was the first to write a gospel. Matthew and Luke followed. Then, John wrote his gospel.

Christ's crucifixion and death must have devastated the apostles. Things did not turn out as they expected.

They fled in fear when Christ was taken captive. Peter denied knowing Christ when he was questioned in the courtyard of the high priest. The gospels say that after Jesus' crucifixion they locked the doors behind them. It is safe to say they were devastated, confused and bewildered.

The apostles must have thought that God was on their side, or at least on Christ's side. What Jesus did, up until this moment, presumably was in harmony with the will of God.

When Christ performed miracles, he often prayed to his heavenly Father. His disciples knew he acted in concert with his Father. Then, there were incidents when the Father's voice was heard, praising and confirming his Son. This happened on the occasion of Christ's baptism in the Jordan River. The Father spoke again in praise at Christ's transfiguration on Mt. Tabor. Peter, James, and John were witnesses to this heavenly manifestation.

Christ's death signaled defeat. Their dreams were shattered. We can only assume that they were plunged into despair.

And eventually, in three days, all this was reversed. Christ rose from the dead. The emotions of his followers were on a roller coaster ride.

His disciples must have been traumatized. It is always difficult to cope with death. Emotions run deep. It takes more than time to adjust to the loss of loved ones.

St. Luke's gospel relates an incident of two disciples meeting the risen Christ. They were on their way to a village named Emmaus, which is about 7 miles from Jerusalem. Apparently they were so overcome with trauma, that they failed to recognize Christ. It was only after a day's travel that they realized it was Jesus. "And it happened that, while he was with them at table, he took bread, said the blessing, broke it and gave it to them. With that their eyes were opened and they recognized him..." (Luke 24:30-31)

Christ's sufferings and death must have undermined the faith of his followers in God. This, together with the love that they had for Christ on a personal level, must have placed a tremendous burden on their hearts.

Their sorrow was compounded by the complete rejection Christ experienced. This is illustrated in the gospels. Jesus was brought before the Sanhedrin as a prisoner. He was falsely accused and condemned for blasphemy. They spat upon him blindfolded him and struck him. Insults were heaped on injuries.

But Christ was put to death by the Romans, wasn't he?

Yes! The Romans permitted the Jewish court, the Sanhedrin, to operate. However, the Sanhedrin was not authorized to inflict the death penalty. Christ was brought before the Roman governor, Pontius Pilate. The charges were altered. The Roman court would not consider the religious charge of blasphemy. Jesus was accused being a king, exciting revolt and advocating the nonpayment of taxes, that is, tribute, to Caesar, the emperor.

And Pilate found Jesus guilty? Deserving of the death penalty?

Not exactly! Christ is brought in chains before the governor. Their dialogue in the gospels is dramatic. Pilate asks him if he is a king. Jesus replies that his kingdom is not of this world. The other charges do not hold water. Nevertheless Pilate feels the pressure of the angry crowd. "Crucify him!", they cry. He may also have wanted to display an iron hand, a firm command, so that there would not be rumors of vacillation and weakness reported to Rome. Pilate washed his hands of the matter. "I am innocent of this man's blood." (Matthew 27:24)

Pilate had Christ whipped, scourged. His back was torn to shreds by leather straps tipped with bone and lead. He gave the orders for Christ to be crucified. These shameful details are related in the gospels. Surely for Christ's mother, Mary, his dear friend, John, the apostle, and his disciples, it was almost too much to bear.

Chapter Twenty-Three

ENCOUNTERING THE RISEN CHRIST

Because of his torture Jesus must have been close to death even before his crucifixion.

It was the Roman custom to flog criminals in preparation for their crucifixion. The soldiers made sport of Christ. "They stripped off his clothes and threw a scarlet military cloak about him. Weaving a crown out of thorns, they placed it on his head, and a reed in his right hand. And kneeling before him, they mocked him, saying "Hail, King of the Jews!" They spat upon him and took the reed and kept hitting him on the head. And when they had mocked him, they stripped him of the cloak, dressed him in his own clothes, and led him off to crucify him." (Matthew 27: 27-31) On the way to Calvary, Jesus was in such a weakened condition that the soldiers made a man, Simon, a Cyrenian, help to carry Christ's cross.

I have heard it said that the Romans commonly put people to death by crucifixion. This is certainly cruel and barbaric.

High on the hill of Calvary, surrounded by a jeering crowd, Christ was nailed to his cross. Two thieves were crucified with him, one on his right, the other on his left. The location was called Golgotha, the Place of the Skull. All four gospels relate details of Christ's execution on the cross. Christ hung between heaven and earth in terrible agony. He spoke from the cross. Seven sentences are recorded. These are referred to as Christ's Seven Last Words. "Jesus cried out in a loud voice, 'Father, into your hands I commend my spirit', and when he had said this, he breathed his last." (Luke 23:46)

Mercifully Christ finally died. There is no doubt that he truly died, is there?

Christ's crucifixion was in plain sight, high on a hilltop, in full view of many spectators. "Now since it was preparation day, in order that the bodies might not remain on the cross on the sabbath, for the sabbath day of that week was a solemn one, the Jews asked Pilate that their legs be broken and they be taken down. So the soldiers came and broke the legs of the first and then the other one who was crucified with Jesus. But when they came to Jesus and saw that he was already dead, they did not break his legs, but one soldier thrust his lance into his side, and immediately blood and water flowed out. An eyewitness has testified and his witness is true; he knows that he is speaking the truth, so that you may [come to] believe." (John 19:31-35)

There must be skeptical people who question whether Christ truly came back to life. They may wonder if there is incontrovertible evidence of Jesus' resurrection.

After Christ's body was entombed, he rose from the dead on the third day. For 40 days he met with his disciples and many others. He ate and drank with them. They touched him. The encounters were many and in different locations.

Meeting with the two disciples on their way to Emmaus was one encounter after Christ's resurrection. What were some of the other encounters?

St. Paul in his letter to the Corinthians speaks of Jesus rising on the third day after his death. "...that he appeared to Cephas (Peter), then to the Twelve. After that, he appeared to more than 500 brothers at once, most of whom are still living, though some have fallen asleep. After that he appeared to James, then to all the apostles. Last of all, as to one born abnormally, he appeared to me." (1 Corinthians 15: 5-8) Paul was not one of the original 12 apostles. The Acts of the Apostles tells of his hatred for Christians and of his miraculous turn-around when Christ appeared to him.

Where did the appearances of the risen Christ take place?

They occurred in or near Jerusalem, in Galilee and on the Mount of Olives. Jesus appeared to Mary Magdalene at the tomb and she went and told his companions. However, "When they heard that he was alive and seen by her, they did not believe." (Mark 16:11) Evidently they were not convinced.

So what happened?

"On the evening of that first day of the week, when the doors were locked, for fear of the Jews, Jesus came and stood in their midst and said to them, "Peace be with you." (John 20:19) He showed them his hands and his side, where he had been wounded. He even ate with them. They rejoiced.

Were all the apostles present?

No! Ten were present. Judas had betrayed Christ. He eventually hanged himself. Thomas was not present when Jesus entered through the locked doors. When the other apostles told Thomas that they had seen Christ, he was incredulous. He vowed not to believe unless he could put his fingers into the nail wounds in Christ's hands. Thomas declared that he would not believe unless he could put his hand into the wound in Christ's side.

Unbelieving Thomas! Is that where the expression comes from?

Yes! But Jesus came again. This time Thomas was present. Christ invited him to touch his wounds, to place his fingers into the wounds. Thomas exclaimed, "My Lord and my God!" John 20: 28

So Christ's disciples became firmly convinced that he rose from the dead.

Their convictions were so deep that nothing would stop them from telling the whole world. The odds were against them. Persecution was in store for them. But they persevered. With the grace of God, they succeeded.

Are there churches or shrines in the Holy Land commemorating Christ's resurrection and his appearances?

There are many churches and shrines visited by tourists and religious pilgrims. The Israelis promote travel and visits. Millions journey to this end of the Mediterranean Sea. But it is well to note that this ancient land has a continuing history of hostilities and violence. Conquerors have come and gone, and new conquerors have arrived. Presently the Palestinians and the Israelis are in on-going conflict. Shrines have been built and destroyed, and rebuilt. The Church of the Resurrection in Jerusalem houses the Holy Sepulcher, Christ's tomb. This is visited by thousands.

What about shrines marking the sites of Christ's appearances?

There is a small, but unusual church along the Sea of Galilee that was built in 1943 by the Franciscans. St. Peter's Church, also called the Chapel of Primacy, is constructed on a large rock. It has an entrance, the rock and an altar. Kephas, (Greek) and Petra (Latin) means rock. Jesus changed Simon's name when he promised to entrust him with the central authority of his Church. (John: 1:42) "…you are Peter, and upon this rock I will build my church…" (Matthew 16:18)

St. John tells of this appearance to seven of Christ's disciples in his gospel. The men were fishing without much luck. Christ stood on the shore, although they did not recognize him. Jesus called out and suggested they cast their nets to the right of their boat. The net snared so many fish that they had to drag it to land. They realized it was Jesus speaking with them. There was a charcoal fire with fish and bread over it. "Jesus said to them, 'Come, and and have breakfast.' And none of the disciples dared to ask him, "Who are you?" because they realized it was the Lord." (John 21:12)

Then, there is an interesting dialogue. Jesus asks three times, " 'Simon, son of John, do you love me? ' " Peter was distressed that he said to him a third time, 'Do you love me?' and he said to him, 'Lord, you know everything; you know that I love you.' [Jesus] said to him, 'Feed my sheep ' ". (John 21: 17-18) Peter denied Christ on three occasions when Jesus was taken captive by the Roman soldiers. Now Christ called for his threefold affirmation. And Jesus entrusted the care of the flock, the Church, to Peter.

Was that Christ's last appearance after his resurrection?

Jesus ascended to his heavenly Father in the presence of his disciples. On the Mount of Olives, overlooking the Kedrin Valley and Jerusalem, there is a rather nondescript mosque. This is regarded at the place where Jesus "was lifted up, and a cloud took him from their sight." (Acts 1: 9) Earlier Christ commissioned them. "Go into the whole world and proclaim the gospel to every creature. Whoever believes and is baptized will be saved; whoever does not believe will be condemned." (Mark 16:16) "...they went forth and preached everywhere..." (Mark 16:20)

Chapter Twenty-Four

WHAT DOES ALL THIS SAY TO YOU?

This is overwhelming. It is a challenge to absorb the significance! A person can live a lifetime and still not have an appreciation deserving of these events.

We do well to ask ourselves what kind of an impact Jesus Christ makes on us. God promised a solution to mankind's dilemma. God was offended by Adam and Eve. All who came after them sinned, too. (Mary excepted) God's solution was to send his Son to be part of mankind. "And the Word became flesh / and made his dwelling among us, / and we saw his glory, / the glory of the Father's only Son, / full of grace and truth." (John 1: 14)

It is clear that God wants to have a relationship with those he created. He fashioned us after his own image and likeness for the very purpose of this relationship. God's ways are far superior to our ways. We attempt to fathom his thoughts and rationale. Why, in God's infinite wisdom, would he resolve the dilemma brought about by our sins by sending his Son?

We try to understand. Our understanding may be limited. But the answers are no longer hidden. The long centuries of the Old Testament are over. We have our answers in what has happened, in what God has done.

God loves us. How can anyone think otherwise?

Saint John is precise. "God so loved the world that he gave his only Son, so that everyone who believes in him might not perish but might have eternal life." (John 3:16)

Our ideas about love extend in many directions. Song lyrics describe love as "a many splendored thing". Is it possible that in the final analysis that all our notions about love spring from God, but unwittingly we fail to associate them with God?

Surely God is the source of everything. As Creator, God brought whatever exists into being. St. John comes to our rescue. "God is love, and whoever remains in love remains in God and God in him. In this is love is brought to perfection among us, that we have confidence on the day of judgment because as he is, so are we in this world. There is no fear in love, but perfect love drives out fear because fear has to do with punishment, and so one who fears is not yet perfect in love. We love because he first loved us." (1 John 4: 16-19)

This is a great revelation. God's love is a great force capable of changing lives.

The insight is like having a glimpse of God, and being transformed.

What happened to Christ's followers? Were they so imbued that they hit the ground running? Did their enthusiasm carry them throughout the known world?

Yes and no! Jesus promised to be with them, even though he ascended to his Father. Christ continued to guide them and to sustain them. He was with them, but in a different manner. When the Father sent his Son, this was a divine intervention in our world. The New Testament tells the story of God's support. The Acts of the Apostles relates the history of the early Church. There is continued intervention.

It would be helpful to have the notion of Church explained. There are so many churches or Christian denominations in existence. Jesus did not merely start a movement from which these developed, did he?

Christ clearly established his Church. He instituted a singular and valid entity. Christ's apostles were not quite ready to "teach all nations" after his ascension. There was still considerable fear in a very hostile

environment. They prayed for ten days. Then, the Holy Spirit came down on them in visible tongue of fire. This was Pentecost Sunday, the 50th day since Jesus' resurrection. This is considered the birthday of the Church. With this grace from God their zeal and determination was unstoppable.

So the "good news" was not welcomed by everyone.

Just as Christ was rejected, so the news of God's love through Jesus was rejected. In Christ's Sermon on the Mount he predicted opposition. "Blessed are you when they insult you and persecute you and utter every kind of evil against you [falsely] because of me. Rejoice and be glad , for your reward will be great in heaven. Thus they persecuted the prophets who were before you." (Matthew 5: 11-12)

How did the apostles succeed?

Slowly and sustained by God! They proclaimed Jesus Christ from village to village, from synagogue to synagogue. They found some receptive ears and willing hearts. "The church throughout Judea, Galilee, and Samaria was at peace. It was being built up and walked in the fear of the Lord, and with the consolation of the holy Spirit it grew in numbers." (Acts 9:31)

What is the makeup of the Church? What makes a church, a church?

It is good to distinguish the word "church" as a society, a family of faith, from a church building. We are talking about Jesus himself constituting a moral body, establishing an institution. In the New Testament the word "church" is mentioned 72 times. Generally speaking an organization or moral body has people who are constituted, perhaps by their bylaws or by a constitution, and there is authority vested in certain members to guide the society. Jesus formulated his church with these elements.

This sounds like the elements that make up a club or organization. There are people, members, who agree to abide by a constitution. They elect or appoint others to speak for them and make decisions for them. A president, vice president, secretary, treasurer and so on.

The comparison is close, but not perfect. The Church has a divine origin. Men and women just do not get together and say, "We are a

church". Jesus formulated his Church. It is a divine organization, not dependent on the organizational skills and efforts who decide to become a moral body.

What did Jesus do?
Christ had followers, disciples. From the disciples he chose his apostles. Collectively he grouped them together as members. Jesus determined their purpose. His teaching and preaching formed them spiritually. They were to carry out his mission. Christ instituted the common means of his Church, providing whatever was necessary to attain everlasting life. The means included whatever was required to follow Christ, to attain holiness, to sustain his members. Jesus granted his own authority to his officials, his apostles, the bishops.

Tell me about their authority.
Peter was Christ's choice be the first pope. On one occasion he asked his apostles what people were saying about him. Peter acclaimed Jesus as the Messiah. "Blessed are you, Simon, son of Jonah. For flesh and blood has not revealed this to you, but my heavenly Father. And so I say to you, you are Peter, and on this rock I will build my church, and the gates of the netherworld shall not prevail against it. I will give you the keys of the kingdom of heaven. Whatever you bind on earth will be bound in heaven; and whatever you loose on earth will be loosed in heaven." (Matthew 16: 17-19) Keys are a sign of authority. The prime authority is vested in Peter. You will recall that after his resurrection along the Sea of Galilee, Jesus told Peter, "Feed my sheep". The apostles shared in other expressions of this authority.

The Church is not a democracy.
Not at all! God does not will it so. Jesus did not constitute the Church in that fashion. But the Church, in its makeup, is perfect. It conforms perfectly to God's intention. Jesus established his Church to last, to persevere through the centuries. This does not imply that each and every Christian is perfect. But the Church's format and constitution is exactly what the good Lord prescribed.

Americans cherish their democracy. They consider it to be the ideal form of government.

We do favor a democracy here in the United States. It is a valid form of government. But God in his infinite wisdom constructed his Church differently.

Chapter Twenty-Five

AUTHORITY

What are some of the powers extended by Jesus to his apostles?

Baptism, the commission to baptize! As well as the authorization to teach! "All power in heaven and on earth has been given to me. Go, therefore, and make disciples of all nations, baptizing them in the name of the Father, and of the Son, and of the holy Spirit, teaching them to observe all that I have commanded you." (Matthew 28: 18-19)

These are important authorizations. Christ's first bishops were authorized by God. We make much of the authorization to teach. Those teaching in schools, colleges and universities are required to be qualified and certified.

And baptism is the gateway to Christ and his Church. Those interested in becoming Christians are taught by those authorized. As catechumens they begin to live the life, and once they complete their training and instructions, they make their commitment to Christ. Christ welcomes the new Christians in baptism.

You must mean that the bishops and priests who baptize welcome the new Christians in Christ's name.

That's true. However Christ acts in his Church and through his priests. "Christ is always present to his Church, especially in the actions of the liturgy. He is present in the sacrifice of the Mass, in the person of the minister (it is the same Christ who formerly offered himself on the cross that now offers himself by the ministry of priests) and most of all

under the eucharistic species. He is present in the sacraments by his power, in such a way, that when someone baptizes, Christ himself baptizes." (Vatican II: Constitution on the Liturgy: Chap. 1 #7)

And what are some of the other powers entrusted to his Church.

The power to forgive! This is to say that the apostles carry on Christ's mission. "I did not come to call the righteous but sinners." (Matthew 9:13) You probably have heard the expression, "To err is human, to forgive is divine." The saying is accurate. Only God can forgive the sins committed against him. Remember that Christ's enemies accused him of blasphemy, usurping the power of God, when Christ forgave people. The New Testament reports Jesus' forgiveness of Mary Magdalene, the paralyzed man and the "good thief" on the cross. Priests and bishops have the authority to forgive sins today in Christ's name. "Peace be with you. As the Father has sent me, so I send you… Receive the holy Spirit. Whose sins you forgive are forgiven them, and whose sins you retain are retained." (John 20: 21-23)

Is this what Catholics mean by "going to confession"?

This is the Sacrament of Reconciliation, or the Sacrament of Penance. Catholics often refer to this sacrament as "going to confession". After confessing their sins, the priest says "I absolve you from your sins in the name of the Father, and of the Son, and of the holy Spirit." Christ speaks through the confessor.

How many sacraments are there?

Seven! Baptism, the Eucharist, Reconciliation, Confirmation, Holy Orders, Matrimony, and the Sacrament of the Sick. These are not new. All were instituted by Jesus. During the time of the Reformation, when there was such turmoil and many Protestant denominations were separating from the Church, some declared their belief only in two sacraments, others in five sacraments. The Council of Trent (1545-1563) clarified and defined the seven.

What is the Sacrament of the Sick?

The compassionate Christ reaches out to the sick and to those weakened by old age. Just as Jesus extended his mercy to many afflicted people in Israel centuries ago, he continues through his priests. "Is anyone among you sick? He should summon the presbyters of the church, and they should pray over him, and anoint [him] with oil in the name of the Lord, and the prayer of faith will save the sick man, and the Lord will raise him up. If he has committed any sins, he will be forgiven." (James 5: 14-15)

Are they all cured? Do miracles take place?

The Church does not teach that miracles occur whenever this sacrament is administered. But the sacrament is a source of strength and consolation. Many who are anointed say that they feel better. Often their conditions improve. If they have proper dispositions of mind and heart, sorrow for their sins, Christ forgives. This is certainly true, especially if they have lost consciousness and had the good intentions to be reconciled to God.

Is this what is referred to as the "Last Rites"? How is the anointing administered?

The sacrament used to be commonly called "Extreme Unction", the last anointing. People do not have to be at death's door. They may simply have a serious illness, or experience debilitation due to old age. The sacrament may take place in a hospital, or in a church where a number of recipients participate in Mass or in prayers. The priest dips his thumb in the holy oil and makes the sign of the cross on the recipient's forehead and on the palms of his hands.

Is this administered in disasters, on the battlefield, and at accidents?

Priests frequently respond to emergencies. Catholics are encouraged to summon the priest when there is serious illness. They are called upon whenever life is threatened.

Tell me about Confirmation.

Baptism, the Eucharist and Confirmation go together as "sacraments of Christian initiation". Confirmation "is necessary for the completion of baptismal grace. For by the Sacrament of Confirmation (the baptized) are more perfectly bound to the Church and are enriched with a special strength of the Holy Spirit. Hence they are, as true witnesses of Christ, more strictly obliged to spread and defend the faith by word and deed." (Catechism of the Catholic Church #1285)

In the Eastern Church all three are conferred at the same time. In the Western Church, Confirmation is usually given some years later following baptism and Holy Communion. However, it is customary when an adult is received into the Church on Holy Saturday at the Easter Vigil, to administer all three sacraments.

What effect does this sacrament have on a person?

A soul is made pleasing and beautiful in baptism. The grace of Confirmation enhances the beauty, making it more resplendent. There are actual graces received. These help to profess faith in Christ and to defend Christ's teachings. The gifts of the Holy Spirit are bestowed in greater measure. There are seven gifts attributed to the Holy Spirit: wisdom, understanding, counsel, knowledge, fortitude, piety and fear of the Lord. (Outlines of Religion for Catholic Youth, Chap. 4, #3)

Did the apostles confirm?

"Now when the apostles in Jerusalem heard that Samaria had accepted the word of God, they sent them Peter and John, who went down and prayed for them, that they might receive the holy Spirit for it had not yet fallen upon any of them; they had only been baptized in the name of the Lord Jesus. Then they laid their hands on them and they received the holy Spirit." (Acts 8: 14-17) The sacrament is conferred by the imposition of hands (and the anointing with the chrism).

In Ephesus St. Paul met with some disciples. They had been baptized in John's (Baptist) baptism of repentance. Paul baptized them in the Lord Jesus. "And when Paul laid (his) hands on them, the holy Spirit came upon them..." (Acts 19: 6)

I am getting the impression that there is considerable challenge in following Christ. Christians experience pressure in being Christians. Is that why Jesus instituted the Sacrament of Confirmation?

Persecution happens in every age. Christians have to carry their crosses and follow Christ. The cross is an identifying feature and characteristic.

Chapter Twenty-Six

SERVING THE LORD

The more we learn about following Christ, the more we recognize the challenges. I'll bet there are more nominal Christians than those who appreciate the full impact of the challenge?

We do not have statistics. Some identify themselves as Christians, but the identification appears to be more in name than in fact. Nevertheless we do well not to be judgmental. Judgment belongs to God. There may be conditions and circumstances beyond our vision. Why do people do the things they do? Only God knows. Still it is axiomatic that God does not allow us to be tempted beyond our strength. And that's why Christ instituted the sacraments to give us the graces we need.

You explain the sacraments in the light of the authority given to the apostles and to his Church. This indicates a different perspective on authority.

Authority and service go hand in hand. This flows from the manner in which Jesus acted. Christ is the Good Shepherd. "Tend the flock of God in your midst, [overseeing] not by constraint but willingly, as God would have it, not for shameful profit but eagerly. Do not lord it over those assigned to you, but be examples to the flock. And when the chief Shepherd is revealed, you will receive the unfading crown of glory." (1 Peter 5: 2-4)

Jesus is clear about authority. The mother of the sons of Zebedee, James and John, spoke to Christ about special privileges for them. "You know how the rulers of the Gentiles lord it over them, and the great ones

make their authority over them felt. But it shall not be so among you. Rather, whoever wishes to be great among you shall be your servant; whoever wishes to be first among you shall be your slave. Just so, the Son of Man did not come to be served but to serve and to give his life as a ransom for many." (Matthew 20: 25-28)

Tell me about the Sacraments of Holy Orders and Matrimony.

The Church likes to point out the wisdom of Christ. He gives graces when they are needed and when they enhance a person's state in life. Marriage and the priesthood bring graces to those who need them. These sacraments are directed in service to others for their eternal salvation. Ordained priests and married people attest to their need for God's help and good graces.

Marriage existed before Jesus Christ came to our world. Why did Christ make it a sacrament?

From the beginning of time God made humans male and female. He said, "Increase and multiply." Marriage is God's idea, his plan for the perpetuation of the race.

The purpose of marriage is the generation and education of children. Mothers and fathers are to educate their children about God. And marriage is for the mutual love and help of the spouses. Husband and wife are to bond with each other. Because of the human condition, the aftermath of original sin, getting along together in marriage is challenging. St. Paul comments, "...such people will experience affliction in their earthly life..." (1 Corinthians 7:28) Jesus elevated marriage to a sacrament knowing well that all spouses need God's graces. As parents they are in special service to their sons and daughters. They are to form their children spiritually through good example and teaching.

This sounds very noble and high minded. But how much of a difference does the sacramental grace make in marriage? There are so many failed marriages, spouses separated and families disrupted.

Standing before the altar and vowing marriage calls for maturity and steadfast reliance on Jesus Christ. Men and women who wed have an edge if they anticipate the challenges. God provides the necessary graces. They must be prepared to enter a permanent state of life. The Church

points out that unity and indissolubility can not be compromised. The traditional wedding promises articulate how totally dedicated the bride and the groom must be. "...for better or for worse, for richer or for poorer, in sickness and in health, until death do us part".

Sometimes we hear young people say, "As long as we love each other, everything will work out." Is that a cliché that does not ring true?

The expression can be quite accurate. Men and women must know what love is and how to live lovingly. There is a difference between genuine love and infatuation. Approaching marriage with prayer and reflection is needed. Seeing life from God's point of view is indispensable.

Have the entertainment and advertising industries distorted life and blurred reality? There is much exploitation of sex. It is pervasive.

God creates human beings with a strong attraction between the opposite sexes. And with good reason! They are to increase and multiply. But their instinct and natural urges are subject to God's will, to his commandments. Purity and chastity are to be observed before marriage, and fidelity after marriage. Good habits formed before marriage, virtues, enhance life after marriage. Morality is determined by God. If men and women do not have God in their lives, they do not have God's perspective about right and wrong. This deficit does not serve them well. The exploitation of sex tends to blur our vision and perspective.

Is that what they mean when they say, "Love is blind".

This is probably a characterization of a person's state when they are smitten.

What do you say to couples who plan to be married?

Pray well. Ask the Lord for enlightenment. Ask the Holy Spirit for the gift of discernment. Marriage is a special calling. Husband and wife make vows to each other. They are to go to God together. God loves them. Jesus showed his love and concern for a newly married couple. At the request of Mary, his mother, Christ performed his first public miracle, changing water into wine. This was in Cana in Galilee. Plan to pray together aloud after marriage. Even before their wedding, praying together is good advice. Attending Mass together, too. They call upon

God for his blessing. Praying together is reassuring for the engaged couple.

They do well to reflect. They are entering a holy state. They will be receiving a sacrament. When two validly baptized people stand before God, before the priest and two witnesses, before the altar, they declare their vows. The priest, who is duly authorized, pronounces them to be husband and wife. Jesus acts through his priest. God unites them. "So they are no longer two, but one flesh. Therefore, what God has joined together, no human being must separate." (Matthew 19: 6)

It should be clear to them that they are serving the Lord. They are serving one another. They serve their sons and daughters in their journey of faith.

Do those who receive Holy Orders take vows?

In the ordination ceremony priests promise to be faithful to the Church and to the bishop. In the western Church those who wish to be priests take a vow to be celibate. Celibacy is not a requirement for those aspiring to the priesthood in the eastern Church. Following centuries of tradition, married men may be ordained.

Why would a man want to be a Catholic priest?

He feels called by Christ. He wishes to follow Christ more closely and devote his life in Christ's service. A priest realizes that he is unworthy of the high calling. But he pursues his priestly vocation trusting in the grace of God.

How would a man know that Christ is calling him?

There are years of discernment. An aspirant to the priesthood consults with his bishop and/or religious superiors. He has the opportunity to receive advice from a spiritual director. He prays for enlightenment. As a seminarian he follows a routine that prepares him spiritually. During his final year of theological studies, he may work in a parish assisting in pastoral ministry.

What are the required studies for seminarians? Do they have to memorize the bible?

No, but it is a good idea. Those ordained must be familiar with the Word of God.

Chapter Twenty-Seven

HISTORY, GOD'S INTERVENTION

Presumably those preparing for the priesthood study the bible. History, too. Church history! You pointed out that the Church existed before the New Testament was written. Is it the intent of church authorities to organize courses so those who are ordained will have a comprehensive picture?

Once a man finishes college he continues his post graduate studies in theology for an additional four years. This presupposes he has taken compatible courses in college. Philosophy is required. Philosophy is termed the handmaiden of theology. The courses may be named differently from seminary to seminary, but basically they are: Logic, Criteriology, Psychology, Ontology, Cosmology, Ethics and Theodicy. There are also courses in the History of Philosophy and the History of the Old and New Testaments.

The names of the courses are intimidating. Their meanings are not readily understood.

Philosophy has to do with studying the roots of things. It is a science of all things seen through their ultimate causes and compared by the natural light of reason. Over the centuries there have been philosophers who developed their own systems. The better know ancient philosophers were Socrates, Plato and Aristotle. A philosopher and theologian whose teachings are studied today by seminarians the world over is St. Thomas Aquinas. A brilliant light of medieval times!

Is all this really necessary for students destined for the priesthood?

The Church thinks so in order to assist priests in meeting the challenges they will encounter. In the early years when Christ's apostles brought the faith to the many nations near and around the Mediterranean basin, they faced similar challenges. St. Paul reflects the complexity of ideas that existed among peoples in the letters he wrote the Corinthians, the Hebrews and others.

When a man pursues the Catholic priesthood and looks ahead to the many anticipated years of study, I'll bet he feels it will never be over.

His four years of theological study include: Scripture, Canon Law, Moral Theology and Dogmatic Theology. There is a course in Apologetics and other courses. His background in philosophy helps in understanding theology.

What is Apologetics?

It is a course enabling a person to prove his religion and its teachings. A priest is called upon to answer questions and to prove the dogmas of faith. Why do we say the things that we say and how can we establish that they are true? The priest gives instructions to adults. He may teach in a classroom or conduct classes for would-be converts.

Most priests serve in local churches, don't they?

There are about 20,000 parishes in the USA. Each parish church is a faith family. Priests care for the flock. They engage in pastoral ministry, preaching, teaching, celebrating Mass, hearing confessions, anointing the sick, presiding at weddings, burying the dead and so on. Local churches are grouped in a larger area, a diocese, and a bishop oversees and presides over the entire flock. Priests collaborate with each other, have meetings, unite in prayer at holy hours. There are annual retreats, spiritual exercises that extend for a few days. Some serve on councils and committees that relate to the entire diocese.

There seems to be considerable collegiality and solidarity among priests and their bishop.

They are renewed and encouraged by meeting and sharing on many levels. Some may golf or play tennis. There are seminars and conferences

that help to update them. This is a rapidly changing world and the timeless teachings of Christ have to be proclaimed. Some priests study in the universities in Rome, the heart of the Church. Others may spend several months on sabbaticals and renewal courses in the Eternal City. The Catholic priest has a unique perspective. He has a sense of history while history continues to be made on a daily basis. Origin and destiny are background for him as he ministers to people here and now.

The priest helps people to find God. This has to bring great personal satisfaction. His ministry is itself a reward. But tell me about church history. Many of us are weak in our grasp of history.
The history of the Catholic Church begins with Jesus Christ. For all practical purposes it started in the Year Zero. Our calendar, the Gregorian calendar,(1582) named after Pope Gregory, is centered on the birth of Jesus Christ. It is helpful to see that Jesus is the central figure in history. We count up from Christ to the present time. (AD Anno Domini, in the year of our Lord) And we count back from Christ (BC Before Christ)

Why is history so important?
It assists us in understanding the present. Genuine history gives us a handle on reality. You probably recall your school days. Remember how the centuries are separated into ancient, medieval and modern history. We do well to observe God's intervention in our world. Church history is not isolated from the other events that have taken place. Ancient Roman history is contemporaneous with Christianity. Remember that the Roman governor of Palestine, Pontius Pilate, was the one who passed the death sentence on Jesus.

Old Testament bible history presumably overlaps and is concomitant with secular history. Give me a short outline. I know Egyptian pharaohs made slaves of the Hebrew people.
The first book in the bible, Genesis, relates details about creation, about Adam and Eve, and what takes place after them. A story that most people know is that of Noah, how the world turned wicked and was destroyed by a flood. Only Noah and his family were saved, riding out the

storm in an ark. The story about the tower of Babel is well known, too. A person can know about those historic times by reading Scripture.

Reading the bible and coordinating the facts is often difficult. It is challenging to keep the names and details straight.

A book by Fulton Ousler entitled, The Greatest Book Even Written, is a simplified and fictionalized account of the Old Testament. It may be helpful and it may be available at the local library. But history is not something we can learn in a day.

Isn't the Old Testament mostly about the Jews?

The bible is a collection of many books. They are all about God's intervention in our world. And the way in which God intervened in the centuries before Christ was principally through and with the Jews or Hebrews. The promise that God made to Adam and Eve after they sinned, the promise that he would send a liberator, or a messiah, came true through this race and this people chosen by God. Bible history and secular history are interwoven. This is the history of salvation.

How does the history of salvation unfold?

Beginning with the 12th chapter of Genesis, we learn about the patriarchs, key figures, in God' plan. Abraham, Isaac, Jacob and Joseph are principal players. Abraham is the Father of the Jews. He was faithful to the belief in the one, true God. God made a covenant with Abraham. God promised him land, the Promised Land, and blessings to his descendents.

Isaac was Abraham's son. And Jacob was Isaac's son. Jacob had 12 sons and these were the fathers of Israel's 12 tribes. You probably have heard the story of Joseph and his coat of many colors. His brothers intended to kill him, but Joseph ended up being sold. He was brought to Egypt and, in time, became favored by the pharaoh. He was instrumental in saving his father and brothers from famine and starvation.

I remember parts of this history, bit and pieces. To put the events in perspective and in chronological order, considerable reading and review is needed.

God works through his creatures. His ways are mysterious. The Chosen People attributed their successes to God. Even though over the centuries some strayed, there was fidelity to the one, true God. They were his people. He was their God. Another standout biblical figure was Moses. He led the Jews out of Egypt. God's relationship with them intensified.

Chapter Twenty-Eight

TIMELINE

What is the timeline on these patriarchs?

Abraham lived about 1900 BC, when Hammurabi was King of Babylon. Isaac and Jacob lived between 1800 and 1700 BC. Joseph lived between 1700 and 1600. The great exodus from Egypt took place between 1250 and 1225 BC. Moses was chosen by God to lead the Hebrews from their slavery and into the Sinai.

The story of Moses and the escape of the Hebrews is fairly well known. There have been movies made.

The serious plight of the Chosen People is explained in the bible. Their numbers increased. The pharaoh felt intimidated. He ordered the death of all Jewish boy babies. The mother of Moses placed him in a basket in a stream where pharaoh's daughter was bathing. She brought him up in the palace. Moses, as an adult, killed an Egyptian and then, fled into the desert. God spoke to Moses at the "burning bush". Moses was to return from exile and to lead his people to freedom. God was on his side.

Isn't it strange how God interacts with people? There is a freedom and also, a cooperation. The decisions are from the people, but they are guided by God.

The bonds between God and the Hebrews developed. Pharaoh was stubborn. It took plagues to convince him. Then, once he decided to let the Hebrews go, he pursued them with his armies. The Red Sea parted so

the Hebrews could escape. The Red Sea then came together, drowning the pursuing Egyptians.

This almost seems like a fair tale.

There is an important happening in this colorful tale. The final, fateful blow that shattered the resolve of pharaoh and the Egyptians was the death of their own first born children. Was this poetic justice? Moses was instructed by God to have his people slaughter a year old lamb or goat and place its blood on the lintel of their homes. An avenging angel would pass over their homes, but take the lives of the Egyptian children in their homes. To this day observe the Jews observe this Passover meal religiously in their homes. This memorial continues to be a key element in their relationship with God.

But the Hebrews were not home free yet. They still had 40 years of wandering through the desert before they arrived at the Promised Land.

You probably remember how God fed them with quails and manna. God called Moses to the Sinai mountaintop and gave him the Ten Commandments. When Moses descended the mountain he found the people reveling and worshipping a golden calf. This appears to be a pattern among human beings.

What kind of a pattern?

There is a seesaw relationship. This has repeated itself from Adam and Eve throughout history. People sin. They stray from God. God is compassionate and forgiving. He extends his loving hand.

And the loving God continues to be with his people.

A significant development took place as the relationship grew between God and the Hebrews. This was the institution of the Ark of the Covenant. Chapters 27 to 37 of Exodus are filled with details of the construction or the Meeting Tent or Dwelling. Moses would pitch the Tent some distance from the people and speak to God face to face. The Ark constructed of acacia wood by a man named Bezalel was 2 ½ cubits long, 1 ½ wide and 1 ½ high. The two stone tablets with the Ten Commandments were placed in the Ark. And the Ark was kept in the Meeting Tent.

Where is the Ark and the stone tablets today?

It is thought they were destroyed with the destruction of the Temple in Jerusalem in 587 BC. At least they disappeared about that time.

So they no longer exist in their original form.

That is a reasonable assumption. However, the Torah, the first five books in the bible, called the Pentateuch, are honored and held in esteem by Jews today. These books contain the Mosaic Law. In every synagogue there is an Ark, not necessarily of the same dimensions. The Ark contains a scroll, a very delicately inscribed copy of the Torah. While God is held to be present everywhere, the Ark is a symbol of God's presence.

What is the difference between a synagogue and a temple?

King Solomon, son of David, known for his wisdom and administration, had the Temple built in Jerusalem. This Temple was destroyed in 587 BC when King Nebuchadnezzar of Babylon captured the city. In 455 BC Jerusalem was restored by Nehemia. Jerusalem and the Temple would be destroyed again by the Romans in 70 AD. The one and only Temple has not been rebuilt. The Western Wall, sometimes called the Wailing Wall, of the temple, is all that remains. Jews gather there to pray today. The area, called the Temple Mount, has Islamic shrines on it.

So today there are only synagogues, places of prayer and worship. Some Reform Jewish congregations may call their places of worship, temples, but they are, in fact, synagogues. Exodus describes an altar of incense and an altar of holocausts as part of the Meeting tent. Burnt offerings, or sacrifices of lambs, goats, bulls etc. were part of the homage given to God in the Meeting tent and in the Temple.

So there are no longer liturgical sacrifices offered in synagogues. Is this significant in the relationship the Jews have with God?

This is something to be noted.

What part do sacrifices play in man's relationship with God?

Sacrifices were offered from the beginning of time. Their purpose is to make up to God for the sins committed against God.

What happened to Moses and the Hebrews after their encounter with God on Sinai?

They continued their journey toward the Promised Land. They met and fought with those already occupying the territories. In the centuries ahead they would succeed and then, be subdued. They would be forced into exile, and then, regain freedom. They would be faithful to the one, true God, and then, worship false gods.

Who were some of the leading historical figures, those involved in the on-again, off-again, relationship with God?

The years between 1200 to 1035 BC is considered the period of the Judges. They were: Joshua, Deborah, Gideon, Jephthah, Samson and Samuel. These were, in some sense, charismatic military leaders. They rallied the tribes to overcome their foes. Falling into enemy hands and being conquered was seen to be a consequence, or punishment, for failing to follow the true God.

And then, what?

There was a period characterized by kings. There was Saul, David, and Solomon. Each had colorful histories. After 935 BC and the death of Solomon, there was a schism. The kingdom became divided: Judah in the south and Israel in the north. There were a series of kings. And the kingdoms came to an end with the fall of Jerusalem in 587 BC. The Hebrews were take to Babylonia in captivity.

Some 50 years later, in 539 BC, Cyrus of Persia conquered the Babylonians. He allowed the Hebrews to return to Jerusalem in 538 BC. Then, in 333 BC, Alexander the Great, conquered and established Greek rule over the land. For the next two centuries or so, descendents of Alexander's generals had control. The Roman general, Pompey, conquered the territory in 63 BC. Puppet kings were appointed by the Romans, including Herod the Great, 37 to 4 BC

This is too much to remember. There were centuries of conflict. But, through these stormy, turbulent years, God guided his Chosen People. It is mysterious how God works.

The Romans were in charge when Jesus Christ was born. Jesus delivered the Hebrews and all people, but in a totally different way.

Chapter Twenty-Nine

CHURCH HISTORY

How did Jesus deliver all people in a different way?

Christ did not lead an army, nor attempt to extricate his people from the control of the Romans. This, no doubt, was the expectation of many since other deliverers won military battles for them over the centuries. It is essential to understand how Jesus was and is the Messiah, the Deliverer. All people from the start of creation sinned and were subject to sin, sometimes even being called slaves to sin. Christ came to free them and to bring them to a perfect relationship with his heavenly Father. Those with limited vision only see the here and now. Jesus deals with eternity. His teachings and his example are comprehensive. They focus on life here on earth, how men and women ought to treat one another, and how they should relate to one another. But they also lead to an ideal relationship with God. Christ is not merely mouthing words when he says, "I am the way, and the truth and the life…".

Well, how is all this played out? How did Christ's comprehensive plan unfold in history?

Our attention now is squarely on Christ's Church. Jesus instituted his Church to guide and direct. We must look back through the centuries and note the significant happenings. Recall that Jesus said he would be with his Church until the end of time.

Does this mean that since Christ is with his Church that everything that the Catholic Church does is perfect? And are you saying that all its officials do not make mistakes?

No! Just as God worked with the Chosen People before the time of Christ, guiding them and delivering them, so does Jesus continue. God works with his creatures respecting the freedom that he gave them. Remember the explanation about the infallibility of the Pope. It is restricted to faith and morals when the pontiff defines for the entire Church, all its members. The 12 apostles Jesus selected were free to follow or not follow. Judas reneged. The others are honored as saints. This is not to demean the authority of Christ in his Church, nor to belittle the authority of Church officials. Their authority is a blessing.

In actuality the Church grew when people began to believe in Christ. Right?

The apostles and disciples told the world about Christ, who he is, and what he accomplished here on earth. They bore witness to his teachings, his miracles, his crucifixion and his resurrection. Men and women came to believe in him, to follow him, to endorse him in their lives. The love of Christ bonded them to one another. Through the apostles and disciples Jesus embraced people. They became his Church. They professed their faith and were baptized. The Church is Christ's community of faith, his family of faith. We are God's sons and daughters.

Presumably the efforts of the apostles began in Jerusalem.

After the coming of the Holy Spirit on Pentecost they journeyed to Samaria and Judea and then, to many other countries. The Acts of the Apostles is one of the books of the New Testament. St. Luke tells of the missionary activity of St. Peter in the first 12 chapters, and then, the missionary activity of St. Paul. They visited the countries in Asia Minor and Europe: Syria, Macedonia, Greece, Rome and so on. The timeline of events extends from after Christ's death and resurrection 33 to St. Paul's imprisonment in Rome about 62 AD. The book was probably written about 70-85 AD. It is said that it was written for the Gentiles. The intent was to convince them that the Christian religion was the one planned by God from the beginning of time. God's plan comes true through his Son, Jesus Christ.

But they encountered hostility in many areas. They were not welcome.

Despite the overwhelming odds, God was with them. The first 3 centuries after Christ are called The Age of the Martyrs. There were 10 major persecutions under the Roman emperors. The Christians suffered every kind of intimidation and threat. They were tortured and thrown to the wild beasts in the arena. Followers of Christ were considered enemies of the state.

How difficult was it for the Christians in Roman times.

St. Peter, the first pope, was martyred. Tradition indicates that he was crucified upside down. St. Paul, the great missionary, was beheaded. St. Cyprian, who the bishop of Carthage (249-258) wrote a letter telling of the martyrdom of Pope Sixtus II along with 4 deacons. Sixtus was put to death in a catacomb during the reign of Emperor Valerian. Cyprian cites a decree of Valerian to the Roman senate "to the effect that bishops, presbyters and deacons shall suffer the death penalty without delay. Senators, distinguished men and members of the equestrian class, are to be deprived of their rank and property, and if, after forfeiting their wealth and privileges, they still persist in professing Christianity, they too are to be sentenced to death. Ladies of the upper classes are to be deprived of their property and exiled. In the case of the members of the imperial staff, any who have either previously confessed and or do now confess to being Christians shall have their property confiscated and shall be assigned as prisoner in the imperial estates." (Breviary Vol. IV, pg. 1297)

And this went on for 3 centuries?

Until 313 when the Emperor Constantine issued the Edict of Milan, granting freedom of worship. Reportedly Constantine was going into battle and saw a vision of a cross along with the inscription, "In hoc signo, vinces", "In this sign you will conquer". He was successful in his military campaign, and this incident moved his heart. Constantine's mother was St. Helen. She was responsible for many of the churches that were built over the holy places in Palestine.

And Constantine was converted?

Yes! He became a Christian. This was the beginning of the Christian Empire. The Empire lasted until the invasion of the barbarians a century of so later. Europe saw an influx of barbarian tribes, the Vandals, the Huns, the Goths etc. The Church proved to be a stabilizing, civilizing influence during these troubling and challenging centuries.

The Church and the Christians must have greatly benefited from their new found freedom. Were they aided by the Roman government?
Christianity became the state religion under the Emperor Theodosius in 380. "It took three centuries for the Church to be accepted in the Roman empire. But by the end of the fourth century Christians had come to believe that the Church could not continue to exist outside of this framework. Civil and religious departments became coterminous; bishops were turned into high officials' it was the emperor who convened councils and so on.

"However, the empire was sick. On the death of the Emperor Theodosius it was finally divided into two parts, and during the fifth century it disintegrated under the onslaughts of the Barbarians in the West. It the East it kept going for another ten centuries, although the area became smaller and smaller. The Church survived all these fluctuations and underwent a deep change." (How to Read The Church, Vol. 1, pg. 116)

So the Church and the state were one. Is this a good idea?
History shows that it made for serious difficulties.

Are you saying that you favor the separation of Church and state?
There are those who favor a complete and radical separation. Let me rephrase the question. Should God and his clear teachings be sanitized from government and its policies? Should elected officials operate on a different set of principles that those revealed by God? Obviously not! Whatever God commands is immanently practical. God's policies make for harmonious living. Nothing can improve on the principles enunciated by the omniscient, all loving God. God's ways advance the unity and the progress of people in society. That having been said, human beings have considerable difficulty in interpreting and applying God's word in governing themselves. Not everybody knows God's revelation. Not

everybody believes in God and his teaching. Not everybody is perfectly motivated, and not capable of embodying proper principles. But governments ought not to be hostile to religion, nor make life unbearable for those who wish to have a relationship with God. Freedom of worship is necessary and desirable for everyone everywhere.

Chapter Thirty

THE CHURCH GROWS

There are many Christian denominations and non-Christian faith communities in the USA and throughout the world. I would imagine the diversity of beliefs and the differences in religions complicate life and policies in a pluralistic society.

Very much so! This dilemma ought to be spelled with capital letters. The Tower of Babel has nothing on world conditions today.

Are Catholic bishops and priests permitted to be government officials today?

The present code of Canon Law says that clerics are not allowed to assume public offices. They are not permitted to participate in the exercise of civil power. (Canon 285 Paragraph 3)

In the earlier centuries did the faith thrive once freedom was granted? How did the Church progress?

The next few centuries (600's- 900's) are characterized by the conversion of the Barbarians. Various chieftains and leaders gained power. There were great efforts made to evangelize them. Monastic life developed. Many of the monks went forth to tell others about Jesus Christ and the intervention of God in this world.

What is a monk?

As the Church grew, some people dedicated themselves totally and exclusively to God. They may have pursued a solitary life, like hermits, or a life in common with others, a cenobitic life. Eventually the monastic life came to mean that folks left the world to devote themselves completely to God in a search for spiritual perfection.

St. Anthony (251-356) is considered the father of the hermits and anchorites of the deserts of Egypt. Later St. Benedict (480-547) who began an eremitic life at Subiaco in Italy, gathered followers and established a monastery at Monte Casino. The Benedictine Rule was embraced by other monks in other monasteries. Benedict is considered the patriarch of Western monasticism.

So over the centuries men who entered religious life, who joined others in monasteries, followed a rule and a daily routine chartered by Anthony and Benedict. From these centers they went forth to communicate their belief in Jesus Christ and his teachings.

They were called upon by the Church to evangelize. Their dedication to Christ motivated them to share their faith. There were also communities of women religious, convents etc. Life went on among peoples in Europe and the Eastern countries. The strong faith of the monks aided the Church and influenced the growth of the Church. We have to remember that there was no electricity, printing presses, or any of the modern means of communication we enjoy today.

The pace had to be much slower. There were no cars, no trains, no airplanes, no supermarkets, no jammed highways and expressways.

We can only imagine what it would have been like if we lived then. There were wars and conflicts. Threats to life and limb existed from warring Barbarian groups. A feudal system developed out of a need for safety and security.

"All that counted were the bonds which people established between themselves by an oath. Land belonged to the warrior who defended it. He put himself under the protection of a more powerful lord who would grant his vassal the possession and administration of a fiefdom or benefice. The social bonds were changed in this way into a hierarchy of warriors and landowners. The Church, which owned large areas of land, was caught up in this system. Every holder of an ecclesiastical office had the use of a piece of land or a benefice which provided him with a living. The bishop was a lord and vassal in the same way as the laity. He had jurisdiction over his land and dispensed justice; he maintained an army." (How To Read Church History, Vol. 1 , Pg. 130-131)

This historical development was clearly a meshing, a blending of Church and state. More complications! How did this state of affairs come about?

The Eastern part of the Merovingian kingdom of Franks was called Austrasia. From there emerged a strong leader, Charles Martel, who took charge of Church affairs. "...he appointed bishops and abbots. He halted the Arab (Moslem) advance in 732 at Poitiers, and then in 737 in Avignon. Holding on to the main sources of power, Pepin the Short, Charles Martel's son and successor, requested Pope Zacharias to legitimate this state of affairs. Pepin and the papacy came to a mutually acceptable arrangement." Pepin had himself crowned by Boniface, the apostle to Germany in 751. Pope Zacharias, threatened in Rome by the Lombards, reconsecrated Pepin and his sons, including Charlemagne. Land confiscated by the Lombards was eventually restored to the pope. "And so the papal states came into being, which were to last until 1870. The pope became ruler over them, but came within the orbit of the kings of France..." (How To Read Church History, Vol. !, Pg. 124-125)

In effect, then, the Church and state were one. Did this come about from expediency?

The element of expediency can not be dismissed. The will to survive is strong. People struggled to survive. The Church struggled to survive. Were the teachings and spirit of Christ embodied in the hearts and minds of all the Christians living during those long centuries? For some, yes! There are saints in every age. For others, no! Some undoubtedly were not guided solely by religious considerations. There were bad laity, bad priests and bad bishops. In time order was restored in society and the Barbarian wanton devastation was concluded. Harsh criticism of the past is best tempered by insight and understanding.

We have books and movies that portray the past. They help us in understanding, but there is nothing like experiencing history. We were not there away back when. Examining the facts is one thing, penetrating the motives is another.

Nevertheless human nature is a constant factor. The more we understand human nature, the greater and more accurate grasp we have on what took place before us. Relationship with God and relationship with others happens in time and in place. The study of Church history is a reflection of the faith in peoples' hearts and how it plays out. There is a tendency to emphasize major events: wars, crimes, disasters, triumphs etc. There is no way of knowing the exact account of souls saved through the centuries. How many went before the judgment seat of God and gained everlasting life through Jesus Christ? History does not have the answer.

And political power has its influence on religion. It has impact on the freedom and/or on the restriction of religious practice. To study history without taking into account man's relationship with God is to pursue truth burdened with an insurmountable handicap.

Yes, and we note a serious breach in Christianity in 1054. This date marks the great schism between the East and West.

What happened?

There was a deep-seated dispute between the East and the West. The Church began with Jesus Christ in Palestine, or Israel, which is that small country at the eastern end of the Mediterranean Sea. The faith grew among peoples in Egypt, Syria, Persia, Asia Minor, Greece...the eastern countries. The faith also grew among the peoples of Europe: France, Spain, Germany, Italy...the western countries. There were five centers or patriarchies: Alexandria, Antioch, Constantinople and Jerusalem in the east; and Rome in the west. There was political polarization in the Roman empires between Rome and Constantinople. There were differences in language (Latin, west: Greek, east), customs, traditions etc. The eastern churches were in full communion with Rome up until 1054. But there was need for reform and reconciliation to bring the east and west together in harmony. Pope Leo IX sent Cardinal Humbert to Constantinople to collaborate with Patriarch Michael Cerularius. To make a long story short, both men proved to be stubborn. They ended up excommunicating one another. And the schism became full blown. This is the origin of the

Orthodox Church. This was the beginning of a division of many Christian churches, not in full communion with Rome.

How many Orthodox believers are there today?

There is an estimate of 220 million worldwide, although many Orthodox estimate more, about 300 million.

Chapter Thirty-One

THE MIDDLE AGES

What is the meaning of "full communion"?

It means there is complete agreement, perfect harmony with the teachings of Christ and the Catholic Church. To express it a different way, Jesus Christ identifies with his Church. Recall how Christ spoke to Saul while he was en route to Damascus to persecute the Church. "Saul, Saul, why are you persecuting me?" In effect "full communion" signifies to be in step substantially with Christ. The Catholic Church considers its relationship with the Orthodox to be almost in full communion. According to the documents of Vatican Council II the Orthodox "are still joined to us in closest intimacy" particularly in the priesthood and in the Eucharist.

Is there hope of reunion?

Yes! There are meetings and dialogues. The lines of communication are open. In recent times there was a significant gesture between Pope Paul VI and the Ecumenical Patriarch Athenagoras I. They mutually nullified the excommunications that took place in 1054.

Have any of the Eastern Churches returned to full communion to the Roman Catholic Church?

Yes! Efforts of reconciliation over the centuries have brought results. The Councils of Lyons 1274 and Ferrara -Florence 1438-1439 were not especially successful, but missionary activities were instrumental in restoring unity. There are many Eastern, or Oriental, Churches in communion: Alexandrian, Armenean, Antiochene, Byzantine, Chaldean etc. In the United States there are thousands of Christians in the Byzantine tradition: Ukrainians, Rutheneans, Melkites, Romanians, Belarusans and Russians. There are also members of the other Easter traditions.

All this happened during the Middle Ages, medieval times. They were not particularly evil, were they?
They span ancient times and modern times. They are in the middle. Good and evil exist in every age, from the beginning until now.

The Middle Ages are often characterized as romantic times, years art and culture thrived, the Renascence.
The Renascence was part of these historical centuries. Also the crusades, the growth of great monasteries, the mendicant orders, the universities, and the easing of the control of the papacy from secular hands. And we can not forget the great schism, when there were three claimants to the papal throne.

What about the monasteries?
They proved to be very influential in the life of the Church. Cluny, founded in 910, restored many of the principles exemplified in the rule of St. Benedict. The abbot was elected by his own monks, rather than appointed by princes and bishops. As time went on there were as many as 50,000 monks in the monasteries of Europe. La Grande Chartreuse was founded by Bruno in 1084. He strove to combine the eremitic life and the common life in the monastery's spiritual routine, along with emphasis on silence and contemplation. The Cistercians came into being at Citeaux in 1098. St. Bernard founded the abbey at Clairvaux in 1115. He attempted to reform the clergy and to Christianize the feudal society.

How much of all this filtered down to the ordinary person?
There was some effect. However the lofty ideals preached and the noble goals of monastic life were not perfectly embraced by the populace in general. To suggest that these illuminating examples were depicted in the Christian lives of ordinary people would be inaccurate. The monks

were the learned ones, copying the scriptures and preserving the sacred books. The people, on the other hand, were for the most part illiterate. Life was different then, more primitive, without all the instantaneous means of communications that we take for granted today.

Tell me about the universities.

In the middle ages intellectual activity was primarily in the monasteries and the focus was religiously related. The early Fathers of the Church were studied. Manuscripts were preserved. The bishops had schools near their cathedrals primarily to educate the clergy. The bishops held the power to authorize the teachers and, consequently, control over curriculum. As the schools grew in number in the cities, there was a restlessness, a desire to escape the autonomy. In 1231 Pope Gregory XI granted that privilege on the University of Paris. The horizon of learning was broadened.

Great cathedrals were built in medieval times.

Artists and sculptors fashioned their faith in stone and mortar. The events of the bible were memorialized in statues and in stained glass windows. Belief in God and in Jesus Christ was expressed in steeples and arches and vaults. Gothic and Romanesque architecture reflected the high esteem placed on religion and man's relationship with his God.

What's the story on the great schism? And what value does this historical happening have on someone seeking a true relationship with God?

The great schism provides fuel for the Church's critics, and perhaps gives strength to their arguments against the authenticity of the Church. The circumstances and events that resulted in three bishops claiming to be pope are complicated.

What happened?

For many years in the 14th century the popes chose to live in Avignon in France. There was heavy influence from French political leaders and French cardinals. There was also support. Avignon was conducive in area and resources for the centralized governing and managing the Church. But there was strong sentiment for returning the Church's headquarters to Rome. Pope Urban V spent three years (1367-1370) in Rome, but then, returned to Avignon. Pope Gregory XI in 1377 was determined to return to Rome and he did return, but he passed away in 1378.

How devastating this wrangling must have been for the people in the pews!

The Italian cardinals made haste to elect an Italian as Pope. He was Urban VI. The French cardinals were unhappy and left Rome. They elected their own pope, Robert of Geneva, who took the name of Clement VI. In 1379 Clement VI established himself as head of the Church in Avignon.

The plot thickens.

At the death of one of the existing "popes", two new popes were elected, Boniface IX in 1389 in Rome and Benedict XIII in 1394 in Avignon. The two new "popes" proceeded to excommunicate each other.

All this extended over several years. How was the dilemma resolved?

The French and Italian cardinals attempted to resolve the situation by convoking the Council of Pisa in 1409. They elected still another pope, Alexander V. But the other two "popes", Boniface IX and Benedict XIII refused to abdicate. Now there were three claimants to the papal throne, Alexander, Boniface and Benedict.

It is easy to see that the 14th and 15th centuries were tumultuous times. The unity of the Church and the unity of faith suffered.

Pope John XIII succeeded Alexander V. He was encouraged by Emperor Sigismund to convoke a Council at Constance (1414-1418). John XIII fled the council. He abdicated. Gregory XII also abdicated. Benedict XIII was deposed. The Council elected Martin V in November 1417. For all practical purposes the schism was over.

Did you say that Jesus promised to be with his Church for all times, even to the end of the world?

The Church survives centuries of trouble and turmoil. Human institutions fade and fall. The Roman Empire is no more. Christ's promise stands. Gales and high waves make the sailing rough, but Christ and his Church weather the storms. The unseen hand of God is present.

Chapter Thirty-Two

REPERCUSSION AND REFORM

Why are you telling me these things? They are certainly not complimentary to Christ's Church.

History is not secret, although the historian's point of view and prejudice surely flavor the telling. Christ's Church is perfect in its principle and in its construction. Jesus makes no mistakes, empowering his disciples and their successors. All the means to holiness are available in its institution. But everyone does not embrace Christ's way. All human beings do not embody the holiness of God. There should be no fear of recounting the past. Those of good heart, those blessed with understanding, stand firm in their faith. Perspective needs to be true. We must see with the eyes of faith.

You mentioned Pope John XXIII in connection with the schism in the 15th century. I thought that one of the modern day popes chose that name.

Angelo Roncali, Cardinal and Patriarch of Venice was elected pope in 1958. He chose the name John XXIII. The "Pope John XIII" in the 15th century is not recognized as a validly elected pontiff.

Evidently the turmoil and confusion of the 14th and 15th centuries had its repercussion. The Protestant Reformation began in the 1500's.

That's true. And we feel its impact to this day. Christianity splintered into hundreds of Protestant denominations. There was discontent. There

was suspicion. There was a feeling that Christ was not being followed correctly and that scripture was not properly interpreted. It was a bewildering time for the ordinary person.

What was done to counteract the damage? What were the efforts made to stabilize society and bring comfort in living the faith?
The Council of Trent that extended from 1545 to 1563 addressed the problem areas. The teachings of Christ and his Church were articulated and defined.

What issues did Trent address?
The Council of Trent lasted almost twenty years. The issues covered a wide range of matters relating to the faith. Among them were: Holy Scripture and tradition, the sacraments, the Eucharist, the Mass, marriage, the priesthood, seminaries and the training of men for the priesthood and justification. Putting these into effect presented a great challenge. The decisions of the Council in Catholic countries depended at least in part on the cooperation of the reigning sovereigns. Since many of the Protestant groups were already ensconced, restoring unity proved to be virtually impossible. It was like closing the gate after the cows were already out in the pasture.

It is certainly evident that there was a great need for reform.
There is a constant need for renewal and reform. In every age there are challenges. Human nature does not change. The general councils of the Church are a response to the errors and mistaken notions that well in the hearts of people. Jesus once remarked that people are like sheep without a shepherd. There is a constant need for shepherding. Jesus is the Good Shepherd.

What are some of the errors that the Church has addressed in more modern times?
In the 16th century there were errors called Jansenism and Quietism. More recently, there was Modernism. And of course, Communism.

Are we all gullible, too quick to embrace unproven theories?

Unwittingly there is a longing in the human heart for God. It surfaces under different forms. We demand perfection and come to expect perfection in other people, in governments, in the Church. When something new comes along, those who are not firmly rooted in reality are more easily lead. Men and women who are aware of their origin, having been created by God .... and aware of their destiny, which is everlasting happiness with God, they are truly blessed. Their goals are defined. Then, if they find Jesus, who is "the way, the truth, and the life", they realize that the mean to the end is within their grasp.

You are oversimplifying.

That's true. But the following is an excerpt from the documents of Vatican Council II which took place in Rome in the early 1960's.

"The world of today reveals itself as at once powerful and weak, capable of achieving the best or the worst. There lies open before it the way to freedom or slavery, progress or regression, brotherhood or hatred. In addition, man is becoming aware that it is for himself to give right direction to the forces that he has himself awakened, forces that can be his master or his servant. He therefor puts questions to himself.

"The tensions disturbing the world today are in fact related to a more fundamental tension rooted in the human heart. In man himself many elements are in conflict with each other. On one side, he has experience of his many limitations as a creature. On the other, he knows that there is no limit to his aspirations, and that he called to a higher form of life."

Who authored that document? It reflects considerable insight.

Who knows? Bishops from all over the world attended Vatican II. They deliberated for about two years. It is speculated that Cardinal Karol Wojtyla of Cracow, Poland wrote some of the documents. And he was elected pope, the 263rd successor of St. Peter on October 16, 1978. He is Pope John Paul II.

Is the Church saying that human beings are searching for God, but do not know which way to turn because of the conflicts within them?

We all have inherited original sin and its consequences. In a sense we are all handicapped. We limp through life in mind and heart. The Vatican II document goes on to say: "Many things compete for his attention, but he always compelled to make a choice among them, and to renounce some. What is more, in his weakness and sinfulness he often does what he does not want to do, and fails to do what he would like to do. In consequence, he suffers from a conflict within himself, and this in turn gives rise to so many tensions in society."

O miserable confusion! And then, I suppose we seek solutions helter-skelter. We begin to follow the trends of the times.

If we think solutions to our dilemmas in life are found only in ourselves rather than in God, we limit our thinking. "Very many people, infected as they are with a materialistic way of life, can not see this dramatic state of affairs in all its clarity, or at least are prevented from giving thought to it because of the unhappiness that they themselves experience.

"Many think that they can find peace in thew different philosophies that are proposed.

"Some look for complete and genuine liberation for man from man's efforts alone. They are convinced that the coming kingdom of man on earth will satisfy all the desires of his heart."

Where are these quotations coming from? They seem to be precisely on target.

The Pastoral Constitution on the Church in the Modern World, Vatican II, Gaudium et Spes, No. 9 & 10.

So, in effect, we are going nowhere without God.

The document was promulgated December 7, 1965, but the answers have been around from the beginning of time. We are very fortunate to have the Church articulate them.

"There are those who despair of finding any meaning in life: they commend the boldness of those who deny all significance to human existence itself, and seek to impose a total meaning on it only from within themselves."

Chapter Thirty-Three

JESUS CHRIST!
YESTERDAY, TODAY AND FOREVER

The document is quite an editorial. It is a timeless commentary. Humans are not capable of lifting themselves up by their bootstraps. They struggle to attain their ultimate goal. So the heavenly Father comes to the rescue by sending his Son, Jesus Christ.

Gaudium et Spes, which is translated "Joy and Hope", goes on to say: "But in the face of the way the world is developing today there is an ever increasing number of people who are asking the most fundamental questions or are seeing them with keener awareness: What is man? What is the meaning of pain, of evil, of death, which still persists in spite of such great progress? What is the use of those successes, achieved at such a cost? What can man contribute to society, what can he expect from society? What will come after this life on earth?

"The Church believes that Christ died and rose for all, and can give man life and strength through his Spirit to fulfill his highest calling; his is the only name under heaven in which men can be saved.

There is power in these words. The Church speaks with authority. Doubts dissolve and disappear. Confidence grows.

With the grace of God it is possible to see clearly. The basis of our belief lies in Jesus Christ. He is the foundation of our faith. "So too the Church belicves that the center and goal of all human history is found in her Lord and Master.

"The Church also affirms that underlying all changes there are many things that do not change; they have their ultimate foundation in Christ, who is the same, yesterday, today and forever."

People do find difficulty adjusting to changes. They often remark how religion is lived differently now than in the past. Some Catholics lament the change in the language of the Mass. Latin was commonly used in worship. Now it is the vernacular, the language of the particular country.

It is very important to know one's religion and to understand what changes and what does not change. Man's relationship with God is alive, active, dynamic. It is not static. When Jesus celebrated the Passover meal on the night before he died, he instituted that most perfect form of worship, namely the offering of himself. He offered himself under the species of bread and wine. On Good Friday Jesus offered himself on the cross. The language of Christ and his disciples was Hebrew or Aramaic, not Latin. Today Christ's Eucharistic Sacrifice is the same. He is the priest. He is the victim. Worshippers unite with Christ at Mass. They worship with Christ. This is the highest form of praise offered to the heavenly Father, Christ offering himself.

We are creatures of habit. We do not like to change our comfortable ways, even in the practice of religion.

There are those who become upset when their beloved pastor is transferred from the parish. This is understandable. Others are discontented when the new pastor introduces lively music at worship. They prefer the seasoned slow and traditional hymns. When the parish church is renovated and some of the familiar furnishings are replaced, parishioners often express their dismay. And this too, is understandable. Sometimes their criticism is well founded. The building is less devotional, at least in their eyes. Nevertheless, all of these changes should not shake their faith in Jesus Christ.

But surely the manner in which these changes take place calls for tact and sensitivity. The better prepared people of faith are, the smoother the transition.

When history is reviewed, this becomes quite evident. There were events and incidents, particularly in the 16th and 17th centuries, that were especially abrasive. These were the years of voyage and discovery. They were times of missionary effort in the "new world". The conquerors brought missionaries with them. There was a search for spices and gold. The Portuguese, the Spanish, the English, the Italians and others sailed the seven seas. European culture clashed with the primitive ways of the natives in the newly discovered lands. Christianity was flavored by a European mindset.

How was this played out?

There are historical examples that illustrate a lack of appreciation and understanding of the teachings of Jesus Christ. These should not diminish the often heroic lives of many missionaries. Evangelization is the essential mission of Christ and the essential mission of his Church. This was accomplished, but it is shaded by those who were less Christian than they should have been.

What happened?

Because of a dispute that arose between Portugal and Spain Pope Alexander VI in 1493 designated discovered lands to the west to Spain and those to the east to Portugal. This may explain why today people in Brazil speak Portuguese and people in the other South American countries speak Spanish. At any rate he left the monarchs of those countries the task of organizing the Church in those areas. This included setting up dioceses and appointing bishops. So the respective kings to some extent were heads of the new churches. So there was the right of patronage. And again, evangelization was tempered and influenced by politics and colonization.

The plot thickens. There is so much history to learn and so much that is not known.

We are only scratching the surface, selecting details to paint a picture with broad strokes. We do this in hopes of being even handed and fair. How has faith in Christ been embraced and reflected in the lives of people? There are outstanding incidents that bear witness to the love of God. There are other outrageous incidents that are blatantly offensive.

Tell me about them.

The book, How To Read Church History (Vol. 2, Pg. 65 No. 187) reads as follows: "The discoverers, the conquerors and the missionaries too behaved in a way which would seem contradictory and scandalous to us. They set up crosses and massacred the Indians. In Mexico, Cortez had an Indian woman Marina baptized before he took her as his concubine. In Peru, Pizzaro demanded an enormous ransom from the Inca Atahualpa, baptized him and then had him strangled."

This is unbelievable. How could those who profess to follow Christ act in such a blasphemous manner?

Hopefully these are isolated incidents. Such conduct may well discourage potential converts to Christ away from him. They undermine credibility in his Church in the minds of some. The world was different in the 16th century, but examples like these are inexcusable. Nevertheless man's inhumanity to man continues. We have the "killing fields" of Cambodia. We can not forget the "Mi Lai massacre". Millions were sent to exile and death in Siberia when the Iron Curtain covered the Soviet Union. These tragedies do not occur when there is love in the human heart.

Love is a great motivator. It is sad that some are misguided in their loyalties and askew in their alignment with God.

There are some Catholic missionaries who are enshrined in our nation's capital because of their lifetime contributions to our country. In National Statuary Hall Father Eusibio Kino, (1645-1711) an Italian Jesuit, represents Arizona. Father Kino labored in the southwest, exploring, communicating the faith and assisting the native Indians in developing livestock and farming.

Father Junipero Serra, (1713-1784) a Spanish Franciscan missionary, brought the faith to Mexico and established nine missions along the California coast. He represents that state in Statuary Hall. Father Serra was beatified by the Church in 1988. There is also a larger than life statue of this outstanding priest near the shrine of Our Lady of Guadalupe in Mexico City.

And we can not forget Father Jacques Marquette, (1637-1675) a French Jesuit, an explorer of America and a missionary among the

Ottawa Indians along Lake Superior. He represents Wisconsin. Marquette University is named after this good Father.

Many of the towns, cities and rivers in this great land bear names relating to the saints and to the faith which these dedicated, sacrificing men represented.

Chapter Thirty-Four

FREEDOM

You refer to places like San Francisco, Sacramento and Corpus Christi.
And Santa Fe, San Antonio, San Diego and San Jose. Faith and country are interwoven in heritage and history.

In the history of the world, of which religion is a part, there are highs and lows, mountains and valleys. There are movements and incidents we are proud of and movements and incidents we are not proud of. Life is a mix of good and evil.
Jesus told a story, a parable, about good seeds and bad seeds, or weeds. An enemy sowed the bad seeds among the good ones. Shall we tear out the weeds? No, was the answer, lest you destroy the good ones in the process. Wait until the harvest and then, you can sort them out. This is like judgment day when God will separate the just from the unjust, the righteous from the sinners.

Slavery has to be a part of our past that we would prefer to forget.
Slavery is not new. The Hebrews had slaves, and were slaves themselves for a time. Leviticus 25:44 reads, "Slaves, male and female, you may indeed possess, provided you buy them from among the neighboring nations." And Moses reminds his people in Deuteronomy 5:15 "For remember that you too were once slaves in Egypt, and the LORD, your God, brought you from there with his strong hand and outstretched arm."

In the conquering and colonization of the New World there was subjugation of native peoples. The development of the newly discovered lands was accomplished on the backs of those who were enslaved.

Forced labor was imposed on the natives in the West Indies. Diseases transported from Europe as well as hard labor in mines is said to have depopulated the Antilles. The Spanish enacted a form of slavery which they called "encomienda", a charge or a commission. Two Dominican priests, Anton Montestinos and Bartolome de Las Casas protested the severe conditions and the imposition of religion. Eventually Pope Paul III declared in a papal Bull, Sublimis Deus (1537) that the Indians were free. They were not to be made Christians by force.

Was it too little too late?

I suppose this could be said about all injustices. But the papal pronouncement did not stop the slave trade. Blacks were kidnapped from the African coasts. An estimated 14 to 20 million were transported across the seas to various colonies. A necessary evil, some said, to benefit the economy. But, of course, unjustified in the eyes of God. The practice went on until the early 1800's. In the United States a civil war broke out, the north against the south. President Abraham Lincoln in the in the 1860's declared the black slaves to be free. The northern forces won out over the southern forces. But true freedom and equality did not become a reality over night. There were restrictions on blacks, where they could eat, where they could attend schools. And there were many other discriminations. The Civil Rights movement of the 1960's was a great step forward. Rev. Dr. Martin Luther King Jr. lead a crusade for justice and freedom. Dr. King addressed thousands of people in Washington, D.C. His words from an old Negro spiritual on the steps of the Lincoln Memorial continue to echo, "Free at last! Free at last! thank God Almighty, we are free at last!"

You are not saying that slavery exists because of religion, are you? Or are you saying that those with religious authority tolerated it?

God created man to be free. Man is fashioned in the image and likeness of God. God loves us. Because we are by nature free beings, we too, are capable of love. And love is not something that can be compelled. God wishes us to love him. He is infinitely loveable. So it is completely

illogical to think God compels us. Jesus invited, "Come, follow me!" Genuine love can not exist except in freedom of mind and heart.

When the explorers from many nations reached the shores of the New World they encountered cultures totally different from their own. The religions of the natives were inculturated and made up their ways of living.
Culture is considered to be a common way of life. People adapt themselves to their natural surroundings and economic needs. In effect it is the way we are in our ordinary living. Sometimes folks refer to culture as something elite, a more sophisticated manner or style. Missionaries have learned over time that it is good to adapt to native or local customs if these do not clash with religious principles or practices. Some cultural practices may enhance worship and liturgy. Drums are used at Catholic Masses in Haiti to great effect.

Nevertheless there is a delicate line between freedom and religious practice. Some practices evidently are not compatible. They clash with faith in practice.
The will of God is the ultimate norm. The Hebrews were commanded not to have false gods before them. Idolatry clashed with the clear line of conduct set down by God. The Spanish explorers discovered human sacrifices in the religious rites of natives in Mexico and other countries. So they attempted to destroy the images. It is said that the government buildings in the grand square in Mexico City, the Zoccolo, came from the pagan temple that existed there. In the 7th century Mohammed is reported to have destroyed the many idols that stood in Mecca. In 2001 there were news reports of the defacing of ancient Buddhist statues in Afghanistan by Islamic zealots. Historians and those dedicated to preserving cultural treasures are outraged. Life is not without its dilemmas.

Despite the challenge and confusion, freedom is not to be compromised.
If you are asking if God is pleased with faith in false gods, or if God approves of idols to false gods, the answer obviously is no. But God respects the freedom with which he has created human beings. Christians, while remaining steadfastly loyal to Christ, should respect the faith traditions of those who are different. Their respect is not translated

into approval. **It is however, a sign of their sensitivity to the faith convictions of others.**

You are saying "Live and let live". In the course of history some terrible things have happened in the name of religion.
Yes! There have been holy wars and crusades. Jesus did not advocate taking up arms. He did protest against the hypocrisy of the scribes and Pharisees. He was strong in his words, but not violent. And that seems to have become the practice and custom in many areas of our world today, "non violent" and "peaceful protest".

This appears to have been the case in the civil rights movement in the United States as well as freedom movements in many other countries as they emerged from the yoke of communism. Governments have been toppled through the collective efforts, the solidarity of peoples. "Solidarnosc" was the cry for freedom in Poland.
There is an old Latin expression, "Cuius religio, eius religio". Roughly translated, it means, "Whose religion, his religion". This may be reflective of the Roman emperors who became Christian following the example of Constantine. The first 300 years after Christ are considered The Age of Martyrs. Christians were persecuted for following Christ. Then, the practice of the Christian faith was eased with the conversion of the emperors and the more tolerant policies permitting freedom to worship.

Presumably this is true when those governing have a particular ideology or philosophy. While communism was philosophically atheistic, it was a "religion" for Marx, Engle, Stalin and other Soviet leaders. There was force used to coerce the people, to indoctrinate them. Churches were confiscated and turned into barns and stables.
Freedom is indispensable for those seeking God. It is a wonderful gift from God. In God's own mysterious way, God invites the faith by the presentation of the truth. Jesus evidences this approach. He says, "I am the way, the truth, and the life…".

Nevertheless truth is not always east to come by. It is elusive. Is this because of the human condition?

St. Paul has some interesting words. "...by the open declaration of the truth we commend ourselves to everyone's conscience in the sight of God." 2 Corinthians 4: 12 He speaks about the gospel being veiled for some... "the god of this age has blinded the minds of unbelievers...". 2 Corinthians 4: 4 "For we do not preach ourselves but Jesus Christ as Lord..." 2 Corinthians 4: 5 Paul hints at human inadequacy. "But we hold this treasure in earthen vessels, that the surpassing power may be of God and not from us." (2 Corinthians 4: 7)

Chapter Thirty-Five

SECULARISM

Was Jesus ever angry? Did Christ ever display his strong disapproval in action?

All four gospel writers, Matthew, Mark, Luke and John, tell of an incident when Jesus challenged money changers in the temple. With a whip Jesus drove them out along with the sheep and cattle used for sacrifices. He overturned their money tables. And the pigeons had to go, too. "Take these out of here, and stop making my Father's house a marketplace." (John 2:16) They were profaning a sacred place.

Were the animals in the temple for sacrificial religious services?

Yes, as prescribed by the Mosaic Law. But the situation was incongruous. The Father's house suffered commercialization. The secular invaded religious premises. Those who came to the temple journeyed from far and wide. Worshippers purchased the sheep, cattle and pigeons on the spot rather that transport the sacrificial offerings from farms or other places. Those who purchased the animals were obliged to use Jewish money, shekels, because the Roman currency was not acceptable.

Is there continued on-going conflict between the secular and the religious? Many today believe it is a good thing to have separation of church and state. Are they inescapably polarized?

Jesus was asked about paying taxes to the Roman emperor. Rome had conquered Israel and the people detested their subjugation and the

imposition of taxes. Christ asked to see a Roman coin. "Whose image is this and whose inscription?" They said, "Caesar's". At that he said to them, "Then repay to Caesar what belongs to Caesar and to God what belongs to God". (Matthew 22: 20-21) Their question was posed in order to trap him. But, besides sidestepping it deftly, he indicated that there was no obstacle in supporting the government by paying taxes.

St. Paul has some interesting words in his letter to the Romans, "Let every person be subordinate to the higher authorities, for there is no authority except from God, and those that exist have been established by God. Therefore , whoever resists authority opposes what God has appointed…" (Romans 13:1-2)

Are we to understand that God does not favor a complete demarcation? A complete separation of church and state?

Secularism is a belief that some people have that religion and church should not enter the functions and practices of the state and/or education. It is a system of doctrine or policies that exclude faith and worship. And we have to ask ourselves should God be excluded from any phase of life or society.

Is secularism peculiar to the United States? Or is it prevalent and pervasive in other countries?

Secularism did not happen overnight. The Church had greater control over the institutions of society in centuries past. Church leaders were also temporal leaders. Toward the end of the 19th century, during troubled and revolutionary times, governments wrested control over civil institutions, education and welfare. There was strong anticlerical sentiment. This was evidenced in Germany in what is called "Kulturkampf", "battle for culture", a series of anticlerical legislations. Similar measures took place in Switzerland and Austria. Clericalism surfaced in Spain. Some religious congregations were exiled, monasteries were pilfered and the separation between church and state became a way of life.

So governments declared, in effect, we can run our affairs without church influence and control.

This was true in France, too. A republican form of government emerged in 1875. Catholics were seen as favoring the monarchy, and were consequently, political opponents. As matters developed the Republicans wished free themselves from the Church's power, even restrict religion to the sphere of private life. They wanted to develop an educational system free from the Church's control.

The end of the 19th century appears to be a period of great transition for the Church.
The Church lost a great part of its territories in 1861. Victor Emmanuel declared himself king of Italy. He was able to accomplish this having received military aid from France's Napoleon III. However, Napoleon kept some troops in Rome, so that Pius IX retained control over the city and surrounding areas.
Vatican Council I began in December 1869 in Rome. This is one of the 21 ecumenical, or general councils of the Church. Ecumenical, the word, means worldwide. Other councils of lesser dimension took place over the Church's 2000 year history. Vatican I adjourned in September 1870. Earlier that year war broke out between France and Germany. Napoleon withdrew his troops from Rome, which were protecting the pope and the Church. Italian troops proceeded to occupy the Eternal City. Rome became the capital of the kingdom of Italy.

So all this is background explaining how the Church changed in its political sphere. This is how secularism developed. And presumably this is a thumbnail sketch of how the Church came full circle.
Jesus founded his Church and predicted that it would suffer. Paradoxically his disciples would be blessed when they were persecuted and insulted because of their faith in him. Christians were burnt at the stake and thrown to the wild beasts in the arena. The Age of the Martyrs extended to the 4th the century. Then, came the Christian Empire under the Romans. Barbarians threatened the Church and civilization itself for several more centuries. Ecclesiastical authority and civil authority meshed and survived for several more centuries, during the Middle Ages, through the years of discovery and missionary activity, and The Reformation.

Where does the Church stand now? How does it relate to governments and to the world?

The Church's headquarters are centered in Rome. The Vatican is a sovereign state. Italy has its governmental capital in Rome, too. Within the city the Church has 108.7 acres, the Vatican, with its offices, departments, galleries, libraries, museums, etc. St. Peter's Basilica is within the Vatican, the largest church in Christendom (with the exception of Our Lady of Peace Basilica in the Ivory Coast). The pope is in command with legislative, judicial and executive powers. The Vatican has a normal population of approximately 1000 people, clergy, religious and lay. An estimated 3,500 people work for the Vatican. The Church has representatives in most countries around the world, and most countries assign diplomats or ambassadors to the Vatican.

But the Church owns considerably less now than it did in the past. The papal estates no longer exist as such.

Pope Pius IX signed the Lateran Accords in 1929, recognizing the rights of Italy and Italy recognizing the Church's rights. The Accords were renewed in 1945 and revised in 1985. The Vatican continues to own 10 buildings beyond its territory, and also, the Holy Father's summer residence some 15 miles from Rome, at Castel Gondolfo. The Vatican has all the usual facilities that other countries enjoy: its own postal system, radio station, publications etc.

Has the Church's influence diminished over the centuries?

There were some who thought the Church would not be able to function and operate without the papal estates. History has proven otherwise. The Church continues to be influential, but perhaps, in a different way. The Church has no army, so it can not enforce it decisions like other governments. The Swiss Guards at the Vatican have had the commission to protect the pope since 1506. There are no tanks, no war planes, no soldiers, sailors or marines at the service of the Church. But there is no doubt that the Church is a moral force, whose impact globally is significant. Jesus promised that he would be with his Church for all ages. Consequently Christ and his teachings continue to extend to the ends of the earth.

Is secularism increasing throughout the world?

It is good to take into account the influence of other religions: Islam, Buddhism, Confucianism, Taoism, Judaism, Hinduism and Shinto. In some countries, perhaps less developed, the customs and traditions are deeply imbedded in the local cultures. Where there are totalitarian governments, religion is often repressed and suppressed. History has witnessed this in Fascism, Nazism and Communism.

Chapter Thirty-Six

SIDE BY SIDE

What does totalitarian mean?

It is a form of government with one political party in complete command, a dictatorship. There is an attempt to dominate, to be totally in charge.

How have the totalitarian governments contributed to the lessening of religion in modern times? Has secularism increased in today's society?

Benito Mussolini and his Fascist party came to power in Italy in 1922. The Church was viewed as its opposition. Many organizations were banned and buildings sacked. Mussolini once declared, "I take a man at birth and do not let him go until the moment of his death, the moment when it is the pope's job to look after him."

Adolph Hitler came to power with his Nazi party in Germany in 1933. His infamous reign is well known. Besides his persecution and suppression of Jews, the Church suffered through anticlerical measures and dissolution of organizations.

Communism imposed its atheistic philosophy in Russia's totalitarian state in 1917. The Soviet Union was formed and proceeded to conqueror and impose its will on Poland, Hungary, Romania and so many other European countries. Churches were converted to barns and stables, formal religious instruction was forbidden, and many anti-religious measures taken. This continued for most of the 20th century. The Soviet

Union no longer exists, but the aftermath of so many years of godless influence left its mark.

Good and evil seem to exist side by side throughout history. Weeds and wheat grow concomitantly.

When Moses went up on the mountain to talk to God and to receive the Ten Commandments, he came down to find the Chosen People worshipping a golden calf. There are gains and losses for God.

Is democracy more conducive to religion?

Neither God nor the Church has canonized a particular form of government. If a democracy fosters and permits freedom of worship, this certainly is a blessing. The United States is a democracy. Its constitution prohibits the establishment of a religion. People are free to worship God. This is good.

Yet dilemmas continue. Not long ago people in the State of Missouri announced that they wished to erect signs in public schools with the slogan, "In God We Trust". They said the motto was on American currency and so the declaration should be allowed in schools. But opponents, The American Civil Liberty Union, the ACLU, threatened to challenge in court.

This has been a pattern in many instances. The separation of church and state is looked upon as a necessity and an ideal. In the United States there are those who see an establishment of religion in some form when support and subsidies are proposed for religious projects or organizations. Catholic schools do not receive financial support, although the education provided to students is regarded by many as superior to public education. Catholics must support public schools with taxes and also, support parochial schools where their children attend.

Do you think that an accommodation will be realized some day? That both public and parochial schools will receive governmental support?

It is possible. There will have to be meeting of minds about an acceptable curriculum. Church authorities must control the decisions about what conforms to church doctrine, especially in controversial subjects. Health, for example. The Church believes that purity and chastity should be taught before marriage and fidelity after marriage.

"Safe sex" is advocated in public schools, the use of contraceptives, and the notion that "you'll know when you are ready to make a choice for sex". This is only an example.

Do governments in other countries support religious schools financially?

Yes! Canada supports Catholic and Protestant schools. In Great Britain, where there is a governmentally established church, The Church of England, a Catholic parish may receive a grant to build a Catholic school. Once the school is built, the government pays for expenses within the school: books, supplies, meals, teachers' salaries etc. The parish pays for expenses on the outside of the building: painting, ground's keeping, maintenance etc. Each parish has a school board with representation from the government and from the parish. In effect, the government recognizes the value of religion.

There have been rulings prohibiting prayer in public schools in the USA. The observance of religious feasts, like Christmas and Easter, are banned. Has the strict interpretation of the Constitution unwittingly contributed to the neutralizing of religion? Has this sanitizing of religion in public education encouraged secularism?

There are many who feel this way. Over a period of time those who attend public schools are influenced. Since religion is excluded, how important can it be? If there is religious practice within the family, students have the opportunity to develop a relationship with God. If, on the other hand, their parents do not foster a relationship with God, then the students are on their own.

Where will the students learn about right and wrong if their mothers and fathers fail to instruct them, and also fail to set an example? How is it possible for students to come to the conclusion that God determines morality?

The importance of sharing faith in God with our children is paramount. If boys and girls grow up not knowing God, there is a great void in their lives. The situation is compounded when the second and third generation of families are secularistically enculturated. Christ's words about "sheep without a shepherd" rings true.

And I suppose when more people ignore God, or consider religion irrelevant, society reflects its emptiness.

A godless society does not have a valid point of interest. There is a lack of a proper sense of direction. There is a need for a true compass to guide people through life.

Presumably it is more difficult in this type of climate for believing men and women to live their faith. Christians experience serious challenge in a climate of indifference and apathy, in an atmosphere where religion is looked upon as redundant.

"Lead us not into temptation" is pertinent in every age. There is still religious persecution in many parts of the world. But challenge assumes many forms. In centuries past folks struggled with the barbarian invasions, corruption among church leaders, interpretation of the bible and suppression of ecclesiastical institutions. Secularism is an entirely different ball game. And when it is built into a governmental system, an accepted way of life, it becomes a tenacious, pervasive subtlety.

What is a good gauge of the depth or pervasiveness of secularism?

There was a time when films and television and/or radio programs reflected the faith of people living in society. A priest was summoned when a character was seriously ill. The last rites were part of the scenario. The entertainment industry has proliferated in productions but the faith dimension is seldom reflected. There are hundreds, perhaps thousands of movies and shows with hundreds and thousands of deaths: war casualties, murders, accidents, and terminal illnesses with the faith dimension ignored or deliberately excluded. Producers and writers have their minds channeled in other directions.

Reportedly one church leader said that American is in danger of loosing its soul.

The United States is a wonderful country. It is constitutionally founded on good principles. This is a great blessing. And it is safe to say that most citizens are kind and considerate. There is compassion in times of tragedy and in times of need. The communication industry does us great service in uniting us from shore to shore. When the majority of men and women love and respect God, they love and respect one another. It is

beneficial when the majority demonstrate their love for God. Faith must be communicated by example and articulated in words...in songs, in books, in television programs...in all phases of life. "In God We Trust" is not meant to be merely a motto.

Chapter Thirty-Seven

GLORY TO GOD

Now that you have explained all this, you must have hope that I will become a Christian and a Catholic.

Ideally every baptized Christian has a yearning to share the treasure of his faith. Jesus said, his followers are "the light of the world", and they are not to hide their light, their faith, under a bushel basket. You are in my prayers. However, faith is a gift from God. Jesus also counseled, "Ask and you shall receive…". Becoming a Christian is a personal decision. Each person must decide freely and willingly to follow Jesus.

This is a serious decision. A life time decision!

It is like the lyrics of a song. " I have decided to follow Jesus…no turning back, no turning back". And you must decide for the right reasons. God's revelation and teachings have to come together in your mind and heart. Christ's words must ring true. "I am the way, the truth, and the life. No one comes to the Father but through me." John 14:6

What is the next step? How do I go about entering the Christ's Church?

Pray sincerely! Ask the Lord to forgive you for all your sins. Pray for the grace to accept Jesus Christ in your heart. Tell the Lord that you believe in him and wish to embrace all his teachings.

Are there classes to attend and instructions to receive?

All parishes extend the hand of friendship. Presumably each parish has the RCIA, an initiation program encompassing several months. (Rite of Initiation for Catholic Adults) If a parish does not have the RCIA, instructions are available. You may have Catholic friends who will accompany you to the classes, or there will be parishioners who will join you for the sessions. Sometimes there are Catholics attending who wish to be updated, renewed in their faith. The classes cover the life of Jesus, God's commandments, the sacraments etc. There is comfort and encouragement in associating with parishioners. They welcome folks into their family of faith. Christ welcomes converts through the parishioners.

When you say a person should have the right reasons for becoming a Catholic and a Christian, what precisely do you mean?

There has to be a conviction that God became man; that Jesus, the Divine Person, is both God and man; that this is the greatest event in history; and that this is God's own plan for man's eternal salvation. There should be a realization that there is no greater love. And a person should want to love God with their whole heart and soul.

And how should the would-be-convert feel in his heart?

He should feel that he has arrived; that he has sought the Lord and found him; that he is no longer searching; and that he wants to praise God; and that he wants to give God honor and glory.

What is meant by "glory"?

A suggested definition is "clear knowledge with praise". A person understands "how great is our God". God is worthy of our praise. In his infinite love God has revealed himself to us. While we are shielded from his magnificence, we are in awe. (No one can see God and live as Moses learned.) Our heart sings for joy, so to speak. The angels had it right when Christ was born. "Glory to God in the highest and on earth peace to those on whom his favor rests." (Luke 2:14) The shepherds in the fields made their way to Bethlehem and honored the newborn Savior.

Catholics sing a hymn to glorify God at Mass, do they not?

The first few words of the Gloria echo the angels' song. The lyrics come from an old Greek hymn. The translation was probably done by St.

Hilary (315-368), the Bishop of Poitiers in France. He is one of the Fathers of the Church, recognized for his teaching. St. Hilary wrote a treatise on the Trinity, among other writings. The Gloria is a joyful hymn. It praises the Father, the Son, and the Holy Spirit. The Gloria is usually sung or recited at Masses throughout the year with the exception of the solemn seasons of Lent and Advent. The feast of St. Hilary is observed on January 13th.

Why is the Catholic worship called the Mass?

The word, Mass, is related to the words of dismissal once used in Latin liturgies. "Ite missa est", "Go, you are sent" is the colloquial translation. The apostles were sent to evangelize, to communicate the "good news". Worshippers in the same way were encouraged to share the gospel, to share their faith in Christ with others.

So, in effect, the word, Mass, is a misnomer.

Catholics are used to referring to the liturgy that way. But the word does not do justice to the importance of the eucharistic celebration. On the night before he died, Jesus offered himself in sacrifice. That was Holy Thursday. The next day, Jesus offered himself on the cross. The Mass is the centerpiece of our relationship with God, the Father. Christ continues to offer himself through the person of the ordained priest who stands at the altar. Those who participate at Mass unite in mind and heart with Jesus. This is the highest form of praise on the face of the earth. Nothing surpasses the glory given to God than this eucharistic worship.

And worshippers receive Christ in Holy Communion?

Jesus is truly present in the Eucharist. As Christ made himself present at the Last Supper under the forms of bread and wine, so he is substantially present in Holy Communion. Communicants are one with their God. "In the institution of the Holy Eucharist, Christ gave us the most perfect, most intimate form of communion between God and man possible in this life, and, out of this, the deepest possible unity between men." (Pastoral Instruction on Social Communication # 11).

Who is allowed to receive Holy Communion?

Baptized Catholics who are in the state of grace, that is, free from serious sin and in harmony with God are permitted and encouraged to receive Christ in Communion. Once a convert is received into the Church, he is urged to be one with Christ in Communion each time he participates in the Mass. This is his greatest blessing. All communicants are encouraged to prepare for their sacramental union with Christ by thoughtful prayer. After receiving Holy Communion they do well to spend some time in prayerful thanksgiving.

Where does the word, Catholic, come from?
The word, Catholic is derived from the Greek. It means universal. Christ wants the "good news" of his gospel to be communicated to everyone on the face of the earth. St. Ignatius of Antioch declared, "Where Jesus Christ is, there is the Catholic Church." Ignatius (50c- 107 AD) succeeded St. Peter who founded the Church in Antioch. Peter then went on to Rome.

Christ is the center of the Christian's life.
St. Paul says, "Christ Jesus is the image of the Invisible God, the first-born of all creatures. In him everything in heaven and on earth was created, things visible and invisible...In him everything continues in being... It is he who is head of the body, the church...It pleased God to make absolute fullness reside in him and, by means of him, to reconcile everything in his person, both on earth and in the heavens, making peace through the blood of his cross." (Colossians 1: 15-20 Breviary I, pg.457-458 AB 1970)

There is great comfort believing in Christ, a wonderful feeling of security. God loves us.
St. Hippolytus said, "Our faith is not founded on empty words; nor are we carried away by mere caprice or beguiled by specious arguments. On the contrary, we put our faith in words spoken by the power of God, spoken by the Word himself at God's command." The saint goes on to explain, "The Word spoke first of all through the prophets, but because the message was couched in such obscure language that it could only be dimly apprehended , in the last days the Father sent the Word in person,

commanding him to show himself openly so that world could see him and be saved." (Breviary I, Pg. 459 © 1975 Catholic Book Publishing Co.)

The End

REFERENCES

1999 World Book (Multimedia Encyclopedia)
The Catholic Encyclopedia
Catechism of The Catholic Church
Webster's New World Dictionary (of the American Language)
Our Sunday Visitor Catholic Almanac 2001 & 1999
Israel Guide © 1972 (Zev Vilnay)
Every Catholic's Guide to The Scriptures (Thomas Nelson Publishers)
Background To The Bible (Richard T A. Murphy, O.P.)
Outlines of Religion for Catholic Youth (Rosenberger & Sugrue)
How To Read Church History (Vol. 1 Jean Comby & Vol. 2 Jean Comby & Diarmaid MacCulloch)
Vatican Council II (documents)
The Sunday Readings (Rev. Kevin O'Sullivan , O.F.M.)
Panorama of Biblical History and Panorama of Church History (Editions L'Ecole © 1962)
Paulist Summary of Evangelii Nuntiandi, TheGospel Must Be Proclaimed.
The Code of Canon Law

PERMISSIONS SOUGHT IN WRITING FOR QUOTES IN *FINDING GOD*

Scripture excerpts in this work are taken from the *New American Bible* with revised New Testament and Revised Psalms © 1991, 1986, 1970 Confraternity of Christian Doctrine, Washington, D.C. Used with permission. All rights reserved. No part of the *New American Bible* may be reproduced in any form without permission in writing from the copyright owner.

The English translation of the writings of St. Cyprian and St. Hippolytus and the Documents of Second Vatican Council from *The Liturgy of the Hours* © 1974, International Committee on English in the Liturgy, Inc. All rights reserved.

INDEX

#

3 Wise Men, 68
40 days and nights, 62

A

Abraham, 11, 12, 14, 15, 24, 26, 40, 124, 127, 158
Acts of the Apostles, 66, 70, 83, 100, 106, 132
Adam, 5, 44, 55, 61, 105, 123, 124, 128
adultery, 23
Age of the Martyrs, The, 133, 165
Aksa Mosque, 24
Alexander, the Great, 18
Allah, 8, 23
altar, 36, 38, 42, 102, 116, 118, 129, 177
Angel Gabriel, 75
angels, 23, 26, 40, 61, 67, 176
animal sacrifices, 37
animals, 7, 163
anointing the sick, 122
Apologetics, 122
apostles, 26, 36, 37, 40, 56, 60, 63, 66, 70, 77, 78, 83, 85, 89, 95, 100, 101, 106, 107, 108, 111, 112, 114, 115, 122, 132, 177
Apostles Creed, 75
Aramaic, 152
Ark of the Covenant, 128
ascension, 95, 106
atheist, 9
atonement, 40, 94

B

Babylonians, 24, 130
Balthasar, 68
baptism, 6, 49, 56, 62, 95, 111, 112, 113, 114
baptized, 33, 40, 53, 56, 60, 74, 103, 111, 113, 114, 118, 132, 154, 175
Barnabas, 70
Beelzebul, 90
belief, 3, 6, 9, 12, 22, 35, 38, 40, 42, 51, 53, 65, 70, 75, 86, 91, 112, 124, 137, 138, 151, 164
Bethlehem, 16, 19, 67, 68, 76, 176
bible, 9, 10, 12, 15, 16, 18, 63, 68, 69, 76, 78, 92, 119, 121, 123, 124, 127, 129, 145, 172
bishops, 37, 50, 52, 53, 54, 108, 111, 112, 118, 122, 133, 134, 137, 139, 144, 145, 153
blasphemy, 20, 85, 96, 112
blind, 16, 58, 78, 84, 90, 117
Body and Blood of Christ, 36
Body of Christ, The, 42
Book of Genesis, 33, 69
Book of Revelation, 57, 69

burning bush, 127
Byzantine, 22, 144

C

Caesar, 67, 96, 164
Calvary, 99
Cana, 48, 117
Canon Law, 122, 137, 181
Capernum, 78, 84, 89
cardinals, 145, 146
Casper, 68
catechumens, 64, 73, 111
Catholic, 25-29, 31, 32, 34-38, 42-50, 52-56, 63-65, 69, 73, 75, 112-114, 118, 122, 123, 132, 137, 143, 148, 152, 154, 159, 165, 170, 171, 175-179, 181
Catholic Church, 25, 26, 28, 31, 32, 34, 42, 44, 45, 48, 50, 52, 54, 55, 56, 64, 114, 123, 132, 143, 178, 181
Catholic Mass, 38
Catholic parish, 171
Catholic priest, 28, 118, 123
Catholic schools, 65, 170, 171
Catholic Youth, 114, 181
Celibacy, 118
chastity, 117, 170
chief priests, 77, 94
Chosen People, 125, 127, 130, 132, 170
Christ, ix, x, xi, 7, 8, 10, 14, 15, 18-22, 24, 26, 31, 34-45, 47-56, 58-70, 75-80, 83-87, 89-97, 99-103, 105-108, 111-118, 122-124, 130-133, 137-140, 143, 145-148, 151-154, 159-161, 163, 164, 166, 171, 175-178
Christ's birth, 67, 68, 77
Christ's disciples, 91, 101, 102
Christ's last appearance, 103
Christ's resurrection, 60, 83, 93, 95, 100, 101
Christ's sufferings, 93, 96
Christ's tomb, 102
Christian, 4, 8, 22-24, 26, 27, 32, 34, 35, 39, 42-44, 46, 47, 49, 50, 54, 56, 59, 64-66, 70, 73, 77, 79, 91, 93, 100, 106, 108, 111, 113-115, 132-134, 137, 139, 141, 144, 153, 158, 160, 165, 172, 175-178, 183
Christianity, 4, 8, 11, 18, 21, 22, 23, 26, 27, 28, 31, 35, 62, 123, 133, 134, 140, 147, 153
Christmas, 67, 91, 92, 171
Church, x, xi, 2, 3, 20, 25, 26, 28, 32, 36-40, 42, 44-46, 48-56, 61, 63-69, 71, 84, 92, 101, 102, 106-109, 111-116, 118, 121-123, 131-134, 137-140, 143-154, 160, 164-166, 169-171, 175, 177, 178, 181
church and state, 163, 164, 170
church attendance, 2
Church of England, 28, 32, 37, 46, 171
Church of the Nativity, 67
civil rights, 46, 158, 160
commandments, 3, 49, 58, 61, 74, 117, 176
Communicants, 42, 177
communion, 38, 42, 140, 143, 144, 177
Communism, 148, 167, 169
condemned to hell, 61
confession, 40, 42, 49, 112, 122
Confirmation, 112, 113, 114
Confucius, 8
congregations, 129, 164
Constantinople, 69, 140
convents, 138
Conversion, 48, 73
converts, 122, 154, 176
Corinthians, 41, 93, 100, 116, 122, 161
Council of Nicaea, 52
Council of Trent, 52, 112, 148
Councils of Nicaea, 69
cross, 14, 20, 36, 38, 73, 76, 80, 99, 100, 111, 112, 113, 114, 133, 152, 177, 178
crown of martyrdom, 66
crucified, 20, 41, 66, 78, 94, 97, 99, 100, 133
crucifixion, 10, 20, 31, 95, 99, 100, 132
crusades, 144, 160

D

day of judgment, 106
death penalty, 96, 133
demons, 90

Index

desire of the flesh, 62
Deuteronomy, v, 157
devil, 61, 62, 90
diocese, 50, 122
disciples, 20, 39, 40, 41, 46, 56, 59, 66, 70, 78, 94, 95, 96, 97, 100, 102, 103, 108, 111, 114, 132, 147, 152, 165
distress, 3
divine intervention, 106
Divine Person, 80, 93, 94, 176
divine power, 83
divorce, 32, 50
doctrine, 7, 164, 170
dogma, 53
Dogmatic Theology, 122

E

Easter, 92, 114, 144, 171
Easter Vigil, 114
ecumenical, 34, 52, 53, 165
ecumenical council, 52, 53
Ecumenism, ix, 31, 34, 43, 44, 49, 54
Egyptians, 7, 128
Emmanuel, 11, 165
Emmaus, 96, 100
Emperor Caesar Augustus, 67
Emperor Justinian, 24
entombed, 100
Episcopalians, 32, 37
Eternal City, 123, 165
Eternal life, 10
Eucharist, 38, 40, 41, 42, 45, 56, 112, 113, 143, 148, 177
eucharistic celebration, 177
Eucharistic liturgy, 54
evangelization, 49, 70, 153
evangelized, 31, 70, 73
Eve, 5, 44, 55, 61, 105, 123, 124, 128
everlasting life, 108, 140
evil, 45, 61, 66, 75, 76, 107, 144, 151, 157, 158, 170
ex cathedra, 51, 53
excommunications, 143
exile, 14, 19, 127, 130, 154

Exodus, 12, 128, 129
Extreme Unction, 113

F

faith, 3, 4, 8, 22, 23, 26-28, 32, 34, 35, 37, 39, 40, 42, 44-47, 49-53, 63-65, 68, 73, 77, 78, 86, 92, 93, 96, 107, 113, 114, 118, 122, 132, 137, 138, 140, 145-148, 151-155, 159, 160, 164, 165, 171, 172, 175-178
faith communities, 27, 65, 137
faithful, 7, 32, 35, 40, 44, 52, 58, 91, 118, 124, 130
false gods, 4, 130, 159
families, 2, 74, 116, 171
fear, 3, 6, 45, 90, 92, 95, 101, 106, 107, 114, 147
fidelity, 117, 125, 170
four gospels, 31, 77, 99
Franciscans, 102

G

Galilee, 60, 78, 89, 94, 101, 102, 107, 108, 117
Garden of Olives, 94
Genesis, 123, 124
Gentiles, 115, 132
glory, 58, 75, 91, 105, 115, 176, 177
God, i, iii, v, ix-xii, 1-6, 8-28, 32-40, 42-44, 46-51, 54-70, 73-76, 78-80, 83-86, 89-96, 101, 105-109, 111-119, 121, 123-125, 127-134, 137, 138, 140, 145-147, 149-154, 157-161, 164, 170-172, 175-178
God's plan, 57, 66, 67, 93, 132
golden calf, 128, 170
Golgotha, 99
Goliath, 13
Good Friday, 152
good news, 70, 77, 107, 177, 178
Good Shepherd, 115, 148
gospel, 20, 31, 39, 41, 47, 60-62, 68-70, 77-79, 83, 84, 86, 89, 95-97, 102, 103, 161, 163, 177, 178

grace, xi, 3, 11, 14, 26, 33, 49, 55-57, 61, 65, 70, 73, 74, 76, 91, 92, 101, 105, 107, 113, 114, 116, 118, 151, 175, 178
Greatest Book Even Written, The, 124

H

Halloween, 61
handicapped, 56, 149
heaven, 6, 9, 21, 24, 25, 41, 53, 55-58, 61, 64, 66, 76, 79, 80, 91, 99, 107, 108, 111, 151, 178
heavenly Father, xi, 14, 15, 18, 21, 22, 26, 35, 36, 37, 46, 51, 54, 58, 60, 61, 65, 80, 86, 91, 95, 103, 108, 131, 151, 152
heavenly manifestation, 95
heavens, 40, 92, 178
Hebrews, 11, 14, 40, 58, 69, 122, 123, 124, 127, 128, 130, 152, 157, 159
heretical, 52
high priest, 40, 95
Hindus, 48
holiness, 1, 59, 108, 147
Holy Communion, 42, 43, 75, 114, 177, 178
Holy Days of Obligation, 74
Holy Eucharist, 177
Holy Father, 50, 51, 52, 53, 166
Holy Innocents, 68
Holy Land, 78, 101
holy oil, 113
Holy Orders, 112, 116, 118
Holy Sepulcher, 102
Holy Spirit, 20, 21, 33, 40, 49, 56, 60, 63, 107, 111-114, 117, 132, 177
Holy Thursday, 177
holy wars, 160
homosexual, 50
Human Condition, The, ix, 43
Hypostatic Union, 16

I

I am the resurrection, 86, 87, 93
illegal, 57

immoral, 57
infallible, 51
instruments of his grace, 84
Isaac, 24, 124, 127
Isaiah, 19, 22, 80
Islam, ix, 8, 11, 18, 21, 22, 23, 25, 167
Israel, 11, 12, 18, 20, 78, 83, 113, 124, 130, 140, 163, 181

J

Jairus, 16, 86, 90
James, 66, 86, 95, 100, 113, 115
Jerusalem, 16, 20, 24, 37, 41, 53, 67, 68, 77, 78, 83, 86, 90, 96, 101, 102, 103, 114, 129, 130, 132, 140
Jesus, x, xi, 8, 10, 14-25, 27, 31, 33, 35-43, 45, 46, 48-50, 52, 54, 55, 57-70, 74-81, 83-85, 86, 89-96, 99-103, 105-108, 111, 112, 114-118, 123, 130, 131, 132, 137, 138, 140, 143, 145-149, 151-153, 157, 159-161, 163, 165, 166, 175-178
Jewish court, 85, 96
Jews, 4, 8, 11, 12, 13, 14, 15, 17, 18, 19, 20, 21, 23, 24, 37, 41, 42, 48, 70, 100, 101, 124, 125, 128, 129, 169
John, xi, 10, 14, 19, 25, 27, 31, 39, 41, 43, 53, 55, 58, 60, 63, 66, 69, 77, 79, 83, 86, 91, 92, 95, 97, 100, 101, 102, 105, 106, 112, 114, 115, 146, 147, 149, 163, 175
John, The Baptist, 10, 19
Jordan River, 60, 78, 95
Judaism, 8, 11, 18, 21, 23, 167
Judas, 20, 66, 101, 132
Judea, 107, 132
judgment day, 157

K

King David, 17
King Herod, 19, 24, 68
King of the Jews, 99
King Jr., Martin Luther, 13, 158
King Solomon, 24, 129

Kingdom of God, 48, 57, 59, 60
kingdom of heaven, 57, 60, 91, 108
Koran, 23

L

Land of Canaan, 12
Last Rites, 113
Last Supper, 26, 36, 38, 41, 177
Lazarus, 16, 86, 93
leper, 84
life and death, 16, 85
light of the world, 175
liturgy, 12, 35, 54, 111, 112, 159, 177, 183
Lord's Prayer, 35, 75
loving homes, 74
Luke, 26, 31, 39, 48, 68, 69, 77, 83, 86, 89, 90, 94, 95, 96, 100, 132, 163, 176
Luther, Martin, 13, 28

M

Magi, 67, 68, 92
manna, 128
Marian Year, 53
Mark, 31, 39, 60, 69, 77, 83, 84, 85, 86, 89, 90, 94, 95, 101, 103, 163
marriage, 28, 45, 47, 48, 116, 117, 148, 170
martyrdom, 133
Mary, 16, 19, 24, 26, 31, 58, 67, 68, 74, 75, 77, 86, 97, 105, 117
Mary Magdalene, 101, 112
Mary's Assumption, 53
Mass, 36, 38, 40, 42, 44, 52, 54, 66, 73, 74, 78, 111, 113, 117, 122, 148, 152, 176, 177, 178
Mass on Sunday, 66, 78
Matrimony, 112, 116
Matthew, iv, xii, 16, 19, 31, 37, 39, 40, 41, 46, 56, 57, 58, 60, 62, 65, 66, 68, 69, 77, 79, 83, 86, 89, 90, 91, 94, 95, 96, 99, 102, 107, 108, 111, 112, 116, 118, 163, 164
means of salvation, 54, 55, 56, 64
Mecca, 22, 23, 159
meditation, 76, 80
Mediterranean Sea, 12, 78, 102, 140
Melchior, 68
mental prayer, 76
Messiah, ix, 12, 13, 14, 15, 17, 18, 19, 21, 70, 78, 83, 95, 108, 131
miracle worker, 83
miracles, 16, 20, 39, 69, 77, 79, 83, 84, 85, 89, 90, 91, 93, 95, 113, 132
miracles of Jesus, 84, 90
missionary, 54, 132, 133, 143, 153, 154, 159, 165
models for life, 75
monasteries, 28, 138, 144, 145, 164
monk, 28, 58, 137
moral body, 107, 108
moral matters, 50
Moral Theology, 122
morality, 1, 51, 53, 60, 75, 117, 171
Mosaic Law, 18, 19, 37, 90, 129, 163
Moses, 12, 14, 18, 19, 125, 127, 128, 130, 157, 170, 176
Moslems, 8, 24
Mount Moriah, 24
Mount of Olives, 101, 103
Mount Sinai, 12
Mount Zion, 41
Mt. Tabor, 95
mute, 90
mythology, 6, 7

N

natural death, 50, 66
New Testament, 18, 20, 23, 39, 68, 69, 70, 79, 80, 95, 106, 107, 112, 121, 132, 183
Noah, 123
non-Catholic, 48, 56
non-Christian, 54, 137
non-conformist, 28
nun, 58

O

Old Testament, 12, 18, 22, 23, 37, 68, 69, 92, 105, 123, 124
original sin, 10, 14, 44, 55, 60, 116, 149
Orthodox believers, 141
Orthodox Church, 141

P

pain, 3, 16, 94, 151
papal throne, 144, 146
parish instruction program, 73, 75
parishioners, 36, 38, 64, 65, 73, 152, 176
parochial schools, 170
Passover, 36, 41, 128, 152
pastor, 66, 152
Pentateuch, 18, 129
Pentecost, 107, 132
Pentecostals, 32, 33
perfection, 4, 18, 21, 34, 37, 57, 58, 74, 106, 138, 149
persecution, 101, 114
Peter, 6, 8, 20, 50, 54, 60, 66, 83, 86, 95, 100, 102, 108, 114, 115, 178
Pharisees, 18, 19, 77, 90, 160
Philistines, 13
plan of salvation, 26, 66
Pontius Pilate, 10, 14, 20, 31, 96, 97, 100, 123
Pope, 25, 28, 29, 32, 37, 43, 50-54, 108, 123, 132, 133, 139, 140, 143, 145-147, 149, 153, 158, 165, 166, 169
Pope Clement, 28, 32
Pope Gregory, 29, 123, 145, 146
Pope John Paul II, 25, 43, 149
Pope Paul VI, 53, 143
praise, 36, 75, 91, 95, 152, 176, 177
prayer, xi, 12, 22, 23, 34, 35, 36, 42, 54, 74, 75, 113, 117, 122, 129, 171, 178
preaching, 10, 14, 17, 18, 22, 65, 84, 93, 108, 122
priesthood, 36, 37, 38, 39, 56, 116, 118, 121, 122, 143, 148
prodigal son, 79
Promised Land, 4, 12, 13, 124, 128, 130
prophets, 12, 14, 17, 22, 107, 178
Protestant, 26, 27, 29, 32, 33, 34, 35, 36, 37, 38, 42, 43, 45, 46, 47, 48, 49, 50, 52, 56, 69, 112, 147, 148, 171
Protestant denominations, 32, 37, 49, 50, 56, 112, 147
public education, 170, 171
public ministry, 60, 78
public schools, 170, 171

R

RCIA, 64, 73, 75, 176
receiving the sacraments, 73
reconciliation, 42, 112, 140, 143
Red Sea, 14, 127
Reformation, The, 165
religious feasts, 171
religious persecution, 172
Repent, ix, 10, 59, 60
repentance, 60, 114
resurrection, x, 20, 31, 38, 86, 87, 93, 100, 102, 103, 107, 108, 132
reverence, 49, 92
Rite of Christian Initiation, 64
Romans, 4, 7, 10, 14, 18, 20, 24, 31, 37, 57, 67, 96, 99, 102, 123, 129, 130, 131, 133, 134, 140, 143, 146, 160, 163, 164, 165
Rome, 25, 52, 96, 123, 132, 139, 140, 145, 146, 149, 163, 165, 166, 178
Rosary, The, 76
rose from the dead, 78, 93, 95, 100, 101

S

sabbath day, 100
Sacrament of Penance, 112
Sacrament of the Sick, 112
sacraments, 56, 112, 113, 114, 115, 116, 148, 176
sacrifice, 12, 24, 37, 40, 111, 177
saints, 57, 58, 132, 139, 155

salvation, 20, 33, 38, 54, 55, 56, 64, 67, 71, 93, 116, 124, 176
Samaria, 107, 114, 132
Sanhedrin, 20, 85, 96
Savior, 70, 176
scribes, 19, 77, 84, 90, 94, 160
Scripture, 20, 36, 49, 58, 68, 95, 122, 124, 145, 148, 183
Scripture scholars, 20, 68, 95
secularism, x, 163-165, 167, 169, 171, 172
seminarian, 118
Sermon on the Mount, 107
seven sacraments, 52, 56
shrines, 101, 102, 129
Simon, 13, 99, 102, 108
sinners, 19, 74, 112, 157
sins, 20, 21, 38, 40, 41, 42, 60, 66, 75, 84, 94, 105, 112, 113, 129, 175
slavery, 13, 14, 127, 149, 158
slaves, 13, 123, 131, 157, 158
Son of God, 40, 70, 83, 92
Son of Man, 41, 85, 94, 116
sorrow, 3, 36, 42, 75, 96, 113
soul, v, 27, 34, 44, 47, 57, 92, 94, 114, 172, 176
Sow a habit, 75
spirit, 25, 49, 89, 100, 139
Spiritual transformation, 73
St. Anthony, 138
St. Benedict, 138, 144
St. Bernard, 144
St. John, 69, 83
St. Mark, 69, 84, 89, 90, 95
St. Michael, the archangel, 61
St. Paul, 7, 26, 40, 41, 42, 57, 66, 79, 93, 100, 114, 116, 122, 132, 133, 161, 164, 178
St. Peter, 6, 8, 50, 51, 95, 102, 132, 133, 149, 178
St. Peter's Basilica, 166
synods, 52
synoptic gospels, 69

T

Talmud, 12, 23

temple, 20, 24, 37, 62, 129, 159, 163
Temple Mount, 129
temptation, 60, 61, 62, 172
Ten Commandments, 12, 128, 170
theology, 33, 36, 52, 121, 122
Thomas, 28, 32, 64, 101, 121, 181
Torah, 12, 129
Tower of Babel, 64, 137
transfiguration, 95
transition period, 74
Transubstantiation, 38
Trappist monk, 64
truth, 7, 9, 10, 20, 22, 25, 26, 34, 47, 54, 55, 58, 63, 70, 91, 100, 105, 131, 140, 149, 160, 161, 175

V

Vatican, 25, 26, 34, 43, 49, 52, 53, 54, 55, 64, 112, 143, 149, 150, 165, 166, 181, 183
Vatican Council, 25, 34, 43, 49, 52, 53, 54, 143, 149, 165, 181, 183
Vatican II, 26, 49, 53, 54, 55, 64, 112, 149, 150
virtues, 74, 117
vow of poverty, 58

W

Wailing Wall, 129
will of God, 57, 60, 61, 95
wisdom, 6, 27, 50, 70, 75, 90, 105, 109, 114, 116, 129
World Christian Encyclopedia, 27
worship, 4, 8, 12, 22, 24, 25, 28, 34-38, 43, 49, 54, 62, 67, 91, 92, 129, 130, 133, 135, 152, 159, 160, 164, 170, 177

Y

Yahweh, 8